Vengeance
Of The
Black Donnellys

CANADA'S MOST FEARED FAMILY
STRIKES BACK FROM THE GRAVE

VENGEANCE
OF THE
BLACK DONNELLYS

THOMAS P. KELLEY

A FIREFLY BOOK

Canadian Cataloguing in Publication Data
Kelley, Thomas P., 1908-
   Vengeance of the Black Donnellys

ISBN 1-895565-55-3

1. Donnelly family — Fiction.   I. Title.
PS8521.E55V3 1995   C813'.54   C95-930387-1
PR9199.3.K45V3 1995

This new edition published 1995 by
Firefly Books
250 Sparks Avenue
Willowdale, Ontario
M2H 2S4

Cover design: Sheila McGraw

Printed in Canada

Contents

To
My Dear wife
Ethel
Born near the old Donnelly Farm

Canada's Most Feared Family Strikes Back from the Grave

It happened, God alone knows why,
In Lucan, long ago.
Dark clouds were on the moon that night,
The fields piled high with snow.
As the mob killed old Johannah,
She cried out with her last breath:
"Your murderin' souls will roast in hell
You'll all know a violent death."

— Old Song —

It happened during the dark hours before the dawn of February 4, 1880, in an icy cold that would have made a Spartan sob. And only God knows why.

It occurred at a notorious farmhouse on a lonely sideroad, surrounded by fields "piled high with snow," while from afar the baying of a farmer's hound intermingled with whistling winds. One of the mobsters said, "It began in blood, it ended in blood," and it would seem that the Donnellys of Lucan had been none too popular with their neighbors; that an outraged vigilante committee had finally accomplished its drastic purpose which—according to *The Toronto Telegram* of February 5, 1880 — had been "to extirpate the vipers."

And how that kill-crazed mob had proceeded to "extirpate!"

Recently I interviewed a very elderly Toronto woman, the former Sadie Frank of Lucan, Ontario, and daughter of the late John Craven Frank. At the age of 15 she had been living in the village when the Donnelly massacre occurred. She told grim stories of midnight fires, mutilated horses, poisoned cattle and bloodshed and, as well as giving the writer a lock of Pat Donnelly's hair, she admitted, "I once had a secret crush on Pat." She told the following story.

"Around eleven in the morning on the day of that awful tragedy (nine hours after it had happened) my eighteen-year-old brother drove County Constable Alfred Brown out to the ruined Donnelly farmhouse. It presented a horrifying spectacle: carnage was everywhere. There were large blood smears on the snow in the yard where Tom Donnelly had been beaten down, slashed and ripped apart by the mob before he was dragged back into the house then mutilated further. My God, it must have been terrible, the work of howling maniacs, and Constable Brown became so sickened by all he saw that he had to throw up.

"By then the house was nothing but ruined and blackened embers, still smoking. The kitchen floor had given way and dropped into the cellar; the butchered bodies of three of the Donnellys had fallen with it into a potato bin. The horrible stench of burnt human flesh and scorched potatoes was such that my brother could never eat another potato in his life."

It had been a slaughter that belonged to the Dark Ages. The sharp knives of the mob had castrated Tom Donnelly before chopping off his head. The kitchen of the house literally swam in blood, where Bridget Donnelly was murdered in a revolting manner; the bodies of four of the Donnellys were so hideously burned and slashed that they were buried in one casket; while the Lucan coroner, Dr. Flock, reported of John Donnelly that, "he had so many shots in his body that he would have had to be cut to mincemeat to get them all out." One story has it that old Johannah Donnelly was scalped, while mob members heated an iron poker until it was a cherry-red. Well, you can guess the rest.

I heard all this years ago from a man whose father had been a member of the mob, and who swore on the Bible that his story was true.

On that long-gone night, all hell had broken loose far out on the Roman Line — the long road that runs by the old Donnelly farm. And the vandal mob had yelled like mad fiends while they fired the house and flames rose over and around the bodies of the annihilated Donnellys.

"Vengeance, by God! Vengeance at last, boys!" the mob's bearded ringleader, Jim Carroll, had shouted. "Damn them to hell, the bastards had it comin' to 'em, and now the fire is eating up the bodies of the Black Donnellys while their souls are roastin' in flames a lot hotter."

Carroll, a burly brute with a face that was hard on the furniture, had shifty eyes, walked with a sway, could scratch his knees without bending and his black hair snapped combs.

One member of the mob, a half-baked farmhand named Purtell, who rarely washed and stank stronger than a mother's love, kept jumping up and down, tickled as hell, shrieking, "Hear 'em sizzle — hear 'em sizzle!" Only a few minutes earlier, Purtell had been chasing the pretty twenty-one-year-old Bridget

Donnelly through the house with an axe, shouting, "I'll bash the young sow's head in." Roaring drunk, as were most of the mob, and aided by several others, screwball Purtell finally caught Bridget Donnelly in an upstairs bedroom, struck her to the floor, crashed his axe against her head, dragged her down a flight of stairs by the heels and helped to slaughter and slash her apart. Her young blood was fresh on the filthy moron's work clothes.

Flames from the burning Donnelly farmhouse rose up like a blazing holocaust, amid a mad, inhuman howling from the mob. High overhead in outer space a shooting star swept across the heavens — falling — falling — falling. Dirty clouds scudded across the moon, while from afar the mournful baying of a farmer's hound went on and on and on.

On the morning following the Donnelly massacre — Thursday, February 5, 1880 — the Toronto newspaper, *The Globe*, brought out in huge headlines the appalling facts that were to shock all Canada — and later the United States as well — facts of what was to be described as "the blackest crime ever committed in the Dominion," one that seemingly wrote "finis" to the longest and certainly the most violent feud in the history of North America. *The Globe* read in part:

HORRIBLE TRAGEDY AT LUCAN
Five Persons Murdered by Mob
An Entire Household Sacrificed
Result of a Family Feud
Thirty Men Engaged in the Bloody Work
The Story as Told by a Child Witness of the Crime

LUCAN, Feb. 4 — Lucan woke this morning to

shock the country with intelligence of the blackest crime ever committed in the Dominion.

The crime consisted of the murder, or rather butchery, of a family of five — father, mother, two brothers and a girl. The victims were named Donnelly, a family that has lived in the neighborhood for upwards of thirty years. They resided on Lot 18, 6th Concession of Biddulph. The farm consists of fifty acres. They bore the unenviable reputation of being:

"The Terrors of the Township!"

On the same date *The Toronto Telegram* informed in part: "The Donnelly family, to a marked degree, bore quarrelsome characteristics — when they were not fighting among their neighbors, they constantly fought among themselves."

This latter information does not come as a surprise, when it is remembered that old Johannah Donnelly frequently said: "From the time they could toddle, I taught me seven sons to be foin fist-and-club fighters. Sure, an' 'tis I who taught them how to gouge, bite off an ear and crack a head with a club; I showed them the best way to send a fast punch to the chin and a good hard kick to the — !"

There is no record of any of the Donnellys ever having attended a charm school.

Even today in the Lucan area, as well as in the surrounding districts, you hear stories which tell that every member of the mob that raided the Donnelly farmhouse died a violent death; that old Johannah prophesied as much as life was being clubbed from her body. Nor are all such stories entirely local. That learned Canadian historian, Edwin C. Guillet, in his

Famous Canadian Trials, Volume 8, writes of the men that slaughtered the Donnellys: "Some people claim that almost all those men eventually suffered a violent death."

Oddly enough, a surprising number of the thirty or so men suspected of having been members of the mob that murdered the Donnellys actually did have a tragic demise; some almost inexplicable. One man, more than a decade after the massacre, is said to have groaned as he writhed in his death agonies, after being gored by a bull: "It was her last words, the awful curse of Johannah Donnelly, that brought this upon me." Another, falling over the deck-rail of a freighter, was pulled out of Lake Ontario, "with a look of horror on his dead features."

Still another, shortly after the turn of the century, is reported to have repeatedly shrieked as, hopelessly insane, he died in a madhouse: "I see her; I tell you I can see old Johannah now! She's come from the grave, she's all covered with blood and she's laughing at me!"

A number of these stories, as well as a series of weird developments and a resumption of hostilities after the Donnelly massacre, are the principal themes of this book. There is also the strange appearance of the beauteous Midnight Lady, that mysterious woman who came from nowhere, spurred on the remaining three Donnelly brothers to seek vengeance, led them on night rides, then finally — .

A former work by this writer, *The Black Donnellys,* which appeared in Canada and the U.S. as well as abroad, described the thirty-three-year Donnelly feud in detail. It began with that May day way back in 1847, when Jim Donnelly, as mean an Irishman as ever left County Tipperary, first arrived in Lucan, Ontario. With him was his scowling, mannish-featured and hostile wife, Johannah, who was later to be referred to as "that gravel-voiced old hellion who caused it all." However, *The Black Donnellys* made no mention of the startling aftermath of the Donnelly Massacre; something that the present volume proposes to do.

Anyone who knows the history of the feud cannot try to claim that the Donnellys were victims of a great injustice. That would be both absurd and untrue. At best the Black Donnellys were a cruel, wild and lawless lot. Detective Hugh McKinnon of Criminal Investigation, who was sent to Lucan to study that turbulent area and cleverly managed to spend a week at the Donnelly farmhouse with his identity unknown, later wrote:

"The Donnellys were not humans, only mad dogs that looked like humans — wild things that should have lived before the cave men. Everyone is bettered now that the Donnellys are wiped out!"

Yet, despite all that, the Black Donnellys had at least one friend, one true and loyal friend, who was none other than the parish priest, the Reverend Father Connolly of Lucan's St. Patrick's Church. On a number of occasions he had pleaded with the Donnellys to mend their ways, but it availed the good man nothing. However, that he was heartbroken by the tragic outcome, is evident by the story of a Toronto reporter who was at St. Patrick's Church on the day of the Donnelly funeral. The article can be found in *The Toronto Telegram* of February 6,1880, under the title of "The Lucan Horror," and describing the arrival of the Donnelly caskets at the church, it reads, in part:

"The melancholy cortège arrived at St. Patrick's Church, and the coffins were deposited in the aisle of the church. At twelve o'clock precisely, mass was cele-

brated by the Reverend Father Connolly, which occupied his time three-quarters of an hour. The Reverend
gentleman then undertook to address the congregation
with which the church was crowded to suffocation. At
the first attempt His Reverence completely broke down,
being overcome by the intensity of his feelings.

"He rallied, however, after a short time, and deliv-
ered an address of nearly an hour's duration. He
turned and faced the congregation with tears streaming from his eyes, and, in a tremulous voice, said:
'Christian friends, we are in the presence of one of the
most solemn scenes ever witnessed. I have assisted at
many solemn burials, but never one like this.' Here his
voice was choked with emotion and after struggling
for a minute he said in an agonized tone, 'My heart is
broken.' Then with his handkerchief over his eyes, and
staggering back against the altar, he threw himself
upon it — and wept like a child."

Four days later, January 10, 1880, an interesting
article by the same reporter appeared in *The Toronto
Telegram*. Written six days after the massacre, he wrote
in part:

"I have just seen two of the Donnelly brothers. One,
William Donnelly, is a most extraordinary character of
medium height, who walks lame, having a clubfoot. His
power lies in his brain. He is as sharp as a steel trap
and possesses an iron will; is determined and farseeing.
The brothers regard the massacre with remarkable
coolness and say little, but their sharp eyes see everything. There is something sinister about their silence."

At the same time a prominent Lucanite predicted
coming events when he said: "The remaining Donnelly
boys won't take the butchery of their parents and
brothers without doing something about it. Even now,

you can be sure they are planning retaliation; hellery of some kind. I tell you I know them; they're taking this too calmly, they're too quiet and I can smell trouble coming. Yes, and death, too."

This book, *Vengeance of the Black Donnellys,* is not a factual account, nor does the writer claim it to be. Instead, it is fiction written around a series of actual happenings; some of which give proof to the old saying that "truth is stranger than fiction." Along with some self-created characters, it has been necessary for the writer to change certain dates and give fictitious names to a number of people to avoid embarrassment to relatives, near and distant, who still enjoy the warmth of old Sol. This I have tried most faithfully to do.

Vengeance of the Black Donnellys is fiction and meant to be fiction. However, the real truth is that this book is based on so much fact — so many of the occurrences mentioned in it actually did happen — that despite all changes and efforts to fictionalize them, it is possible that a few old-timers around Lucan — who are familiar with the strange aftermath of the Donnelly feud, will be able, in the following pages, by putting two and two together, to read between the lines.

T.P.K.

VENGEANCE

OF THE

BLACK DONNELLYS

The terrible Donnelly feud began in the spring of 1847, only a few hours after James Donnelly, an Irish immigrant, first arrived in Lucan from his native Tipperary. For sheer savagery, the notorious Hatfield-McCoy feud and the lawless exploits of Jesse James were Victorian tea parties compared to Donnelly exploits.

CHAPTER ONE

The Old Man in the Graveyard

Then as the shades of night draw nigh,
While parents quail and children cry.
The ghosts of the Donnellys still ride by,
Out on the Roman Line.
— Old Song —

With the setting sun a golden bonfire, the sleek road-ster with the Ohio licence plate wheeled off a Cana-dian highway and purred down a sideroad till it pulled up and braked before a quiet country churchyard. An aroma of freshly cut hay came from the surrounding fields; the almost sepulchral stillness was broken only by the lowing of cattle on a hillside and the chirping of starlings who soared and dove in the blueness above trees lining the road. Overhead, evening clouds were sculptured in the sky.

A mile away was the small village of Lucan, Ontario. The same once grim Lucan that had been known as "the wildest spot in Canada." But those violent days, long gone, were now only memories. Just terrible memories.

The couple who left the car to enter the graveyard, both in their mid-twenties, were a striking pair. Ann

3

Graham was blonde, shapely and pretty; her husband a strapping six-footer with clean-cut features. For some minutes the two advanced slowly and erratically past time-ravaged crosses and headstones. It was evident that they were searching for some particular plot, that they were strangers to their surroundings and were experiencing that sensation of awe which one invariably feels in a deserted graveyard. It was the young wife who presently called out:

"Here it is, Don; right over here. The tombstone of the Black Donnellys."

Don Graham, reading the inscription on the lichen-spotted headstone, straightened up and a smile lit his handsome face. "Trust Ann to find it. Good girl," he congratulated.

And so they came to the final resting spot of what had once been the most feared family in the history of the vast Dominion of Canada. The Black Donnellys!

Standing before the red granite tombstone in a lonely graveyard a mile from the village of Lucan, the Grahams spent the next few minutes reading the inscription chiseled upon it; words which stated baldly that six members of the terrible Donnelly family had been "MURDERED." On the far side of the pillar-like structure the young couple found the grave of Mike Donnelly, who died from a knife in the back while he was savagely beating a man to death with his bare hands. Then, as they continued to circle the tombstone, they came to the inscription on the right side which caused Ann Graham to exclaim:

"Why, here is the grave of William Donnelly. But — but I did not know that he was buried here." She turned to her husband. "You remember reading about William Donnelly? The one that had the clubfoot?"

The other nodded. "Yes, the book told that William was supposed to be the most cunning and cruel of the Donnellys; that he masterminded their night rides and that the enemies of the family frequently referred to him as the worst of the whole damn lot." He chuckled, then added, "And that was certainly saying a lot."

"What do you mean, Don?"

"I'm putting it right on the line; I'm saying that the Donnellys were a bad bunch and deserved what they got."

"Well at least William was not murdered," she reminded him.

"True; but his was an exceptional case, that is, as far as a Donnelly was concerned. For some reason justice didn't catch up with him; he died with his boots off and in bed."

"Which is as it should be," came her practical answer.

"Which is as it rarely was, back in those days when that damn Donnelly family so terrorized this district."

Ann started to make some reply when a flapping of wings raised her eyes skyward. There, forty feet above her head, its wings loudly churning the air, was a huge coal-black crow; by far the largest she had ever seen. Where it had come from she had no way of knowing, nor had there been anything to herald its appearance; suddenly it was above her and that was that. Even as she watched, it twice encircled the small graveyard, cawing loudly, then slowly winging lower and lower, finally coming to rest on the top of a nearby headstone. The crow added a touch of the macabre to that silent village of the dead. Another rasping "caw" stabbed from its throat, then its beady little eyes regarded the two visitors with what Ann Graham decided was a most hostile glare.

Their gaze met and held, then the pretty American girl exclaimed: "Stop looking at us like that. Fly away, crow!"

The answer was another loud "Caw!"

Exasperated, she stamped her foot. "Go — fly away!"

But from its morbid perch the coal-black bird continued to watch her in what seemed to her an eerie silence and a phantom-like hate. Of course it could have been her surroundings that caused her to feel a slight fear; yet there was also an inexplicable something which whispered that all was not well — that her fear was caused by something uncanny. Puzzled, she turned to her husband who, engrossed in reading the grim inscriptions on the Donnelly tombstone, was unaware of the bird's presence. For a moment she watched him, then said:

"Don, do you see the strange way that bird is glaring at us!"

"Huh?"

She began again. "That crow over there — ."

He turned. "What was that you said? Something about a crow?"

"Right behind us on that tall headstone near the fence. Notice the odd way that the crow sitting upon it is glaring at us. As though he hates us for being here; as though we were grave robbers or something." She shuddered. "He's giving me the creeps."

Looking at her husband, she saw his gaze follow the gesture of her arm. "What in the world are you talking about, Ann?"

"About that crow on the headstone near the fence."

"But there isn't any crow on that headstone or any other." Slightly bewildered, he turned to her, "What's the matter, dear? Aren't you feeling well?"

Ann Graham wheeled to the headstone, to find it was minus one crow. Yes, though she had seen it a few seconds earlier and there had been no flutter of wings to announce its departure, the strange bird that seemingly came from nowhere, had just as mysteriously vanished — utterly vanished. And apparently back to nowhere!

"A pleasant good evening to you both. I saw your car at the gateway, noticed the licence and said to myself that some more Americans have journeyed up here to see the grave of the Donnellys. It attracts quite a few visitors from across the border."

Ann and Don Graham turned to learn the identify of the speaker.

It was a tall and erect, though a very aged man who stood before them; one whose swarthy features were grizzled and seared by time. Leaning on the blackthorn stick, he was clothed in rural apparel — toil-smeared trousers and blue work-shirt — while a battered black hat was pushed far back on thick, wavy, snow-white hair. But for all his rough appearance, the passing years had failed to erase traces of a handsome face, or a certain defiant mannerism, a devil-may-care bearing that was as an open challenge to danger. Their eyes met, and he added:

"As I walked up I noticed you were both interested in that headstone near the fence. Is it so different from the others?"

Don Graham spoke up. "No, but my wife claims she saw a large crow perched on it; yet if you can see one, will you tell me where it is or —."

"Don, I tell you I did!" she broke in. "He was sitting

right on that headstone, large as life, glaring at us, wicked-looking and evil. Then my eyes strayed only for seconds while I called your attention to him, and when I looked again he was gone." She snapped two fingers, "Vanished like that. I tell you, there is something very strange about it. Birds don't just disappear into thin air and I know what I saw."

Her husband started to make some reply, thought better of it and turned to the stranger. "I'm Don Graham of Dayton, Ohio," he said. "This is my wife, Ann, and you are quite right; we did drive up here to see the Donnelly tombstone."

The old man nodded. "Have you seen the old Donnelly farm?" he asked. "It is just a few miles up the road and was once the scene of an appalling tragedy, the conclusion of an era of violence without equal on the North American continent, the climax of a thirty-three-year feud that began in blood and ended in blood."

"So I understand," answered Graham, "and we intend to see it tomorrow. From here we drive back to the hotel in London, where we are staying, but will return in the morning. We plan to make a day of it, to take in all the places connected with that terrible feud."

Ann Graham's interest in the stranger caused her to forget the recent mystery of the vanishing crow. "Tell me," she asked, "have you lived around here for quite a while?"

A smile flitted across the aged features; it was evident that in some way her question amused him. A slight pause followed, while from afar came the drawn out whistle of an evening train. Both Ann and her husband noted that despite his apparent age, the voice of the stranger was that of a much younger man — clear, well modulated and even.

"Yes, I've lived here a great number of years; practically all my life and it has been a far longer one than any other in this district."

"Then as a boy you may have seen some of the Donnellys!" exclaimed Ann. "You might even have known a few of them."

"I knew all of them, perhaps better than anyone ever did, and I was more than a boy at the time," came the reply, his words affirmed with another nod. "Yes, I knew them all; old Jim Donnelly, his wife, Johannah, their seven wild sons and their pretty daughter Jennie. Ah, yes, beautiful, blue-eyed Jennie, whose laughter was like distant sleighbells and who was once the belle of the district."

The blackthorn stick waved to the nearby church beyond the graveyard fence, a church that had known a tread of rural parishioners for over a century.

"There was that time, over eighty years ago," he went on, "when I saw Jennie Donnelly in that church, dressed in black and weeping during the funeral services for the slaughtered members of her family. She was with her remaining brothers. I sat near her, I heard her sobs. Yes, and it was on the same day, and on the very road you see before the church, when began the strange and little known story that was to follow."

"We learned of Jennie in the book, *The Black Donnellys,*" said Don Graham. "We both read it in Dayton, Ohio. We became interested in the story of the feud and when vacation time rolled around, Ann and I decided to drive up here and see where it had happened."

"I thought as much," was the old man's answer. "During the years following the Donnelly feud, the outside world gradually forgot about it. Then, a few years ago, someone came this way, delved into our old records and legends, and wrote the book about the violent period this district had once known. This has brought many curious visitors from near and far to the Lucan area."

"But tourists coming into this district or any other spend money in it," reminded Don Graham. "Surely there is nothing wrong with that."

"Absolutely nothing wrong with it; any added revenue around here is welcome," agreed the other. "But if a book had to be written on the Donnellys, why didn't it tell the whole story? Why didn't it mention what happened after the Donnelly massacre, so that folks would know all that really happened, learn the facts behind the massacre and how, in a sense, it was the dead Donnellys themselves who finally won?"

Again that strange smile swept across his face, like a brief glow of triumph, before he continued.

"For it was the Donnellys who finally did win, you know." And his voice rose in elation. "Yes, it was the Donnellys who eventually won, even though old records tell otherwise and you will find no mention of their victory in any book or archive, since I alone know the story of what happened after the massacre."

He struck the ground with his stick to emphasize his point.

"And it is a true story, though an almost unbelievable one of terror, violence, wailing winds and a beautiful woman whose features were masked, who rode a black horse through swirling fogs and darkness, then always vanished with the dawn. The story of a weird love that lasted throughout the years, and a final vengeance and triumph that was gained for those beyond the grave."

That did it!

Five minutes later the man with the snow-white hair was seated on a patch of grass beside the Donnelly tombstone, while nearby sat the young American couple. They were determined to hear the story; Ann Graham proved to be as persuasive as she was pretty while her husband, having driven hundreds of miles to sate his curiosity, welcomed a chance to hear "a strange and little known story" about the Black Donnellys.

The old man put up a few half-hearted protests, pointing out that the afternoon was nearly gone; reminding them that the story would take some time in the telling and dusk would be upon them before its conclusion. But they overruled his excuses; they said that time meant nothing to them.

"You just have to tell us that story, sir," said Ann, while her husband added, "And when you have finished, we will take you home in plenty of time for your evening meal, or better still, we can all drive into Lucan and have supper together. I understand there are still several buildings there that have known the tread of Donnelly footsteps."

The answer was a quiet chuckle of resignation, while the old man removed his hat and wiped his forehead with the back of one hand. Then he produced and lit a pipe at the expense of three matches; more seconds ticked along while he adjusted himself to a comfortable position, but presently he was saying:

"So you want to hear the strange story of the vengeance of the Black Donnellys?" He shrugged, "Well, why not, though you have my promise that in the nearly eighty years since it happened I have never

told it to anybody else. But now that I think of it, perhaps it should be told. After all, I do not expect to be
in this world much longer and maybe I should break
my long silence and leave the story with those who will
tell others who, in turn, will pass it on to others, till
eventually it may be known in the outside world that it
was the Donnellys who finally won."

As the Grahams watched, his eyes went to the nearby trees, then to the blueness overhead, while a deep
sigh escaped him.

"A lovely evening," were his next words, "and
though I have known many thousands of sundowns, I
always find something new and wonderful in every one
of them." He smiled. "You know, I sometimes think that
the hour of sundown, coming as it does just before darkness, is for the sole purpose of reminding us of the beau-
ties of a world that will soon be vanishing into the shades
of night. To me, sundown is a golden benediction; like
the few brief moments of peace and spiritual comfort
that a dying and repentant sinner might know in the
quiet of a wayside chapel before death overtakes him."

Listening to him, the young American couple were
of the opinion that the speaker was no ordinary rural
inhabitant such as one might expect to find in the district. There was that — well, there was something about
him that was different, though neither of the Grahams
could decided just what it was. And he was endowed
with that rare quality of being able to convince others
that every word he spoke was gospel truth. He was
clean shaven, his eyes were clear and piercing.

"Here is a man who lived in the reign of the
Donnelly feud, and knew stark horror in the raw,"
thought Don Graham; "One who has doubtlessly seen,
many times, the distant flare of burning farmhouses that

were set aflame by the terrible Donnellys. He admits to seeing them; he might have occasionally heard, from the darkness, the din of their galloping horses, and even their wild shouts of triumph that screeched through the night and terrorized their enemies as they rode away from some newly perpetrated vandalism while the surrounding countryside trembled and prayed for dawn!"

But aloud Don Graham said: "You were going to tell us of how the Black Donnellys struck back at their enemies from the grave."

The old man nodded.

"I said I would," was his reply. "A promise is something I have yet to violate, and where could I find a more appropriate spot to tell the story than in this very graveyard, where lie the remains of so many who knew the violence and terror of the Donnellys. It is needless to tell of what led up to the Donnelly massacre, since you both have read the book about the feud and are familiar with the facts — at least with most of them. Ah, but it is what happened after the massacre and the seeming triumph of the enemies of the Donnellys that concern us now."

Again his blackthorn stick gestured towards the church.

"And, oddly enough, it was on this very road that the first of a series of incidents began which was to bring about the following story. Yes, young people, it all started right here; right here while the gods of irony must have smiled as they awaited the outcome."

Then, as he went on Ann and Don Graham found themselves drifting back into time and that grim and little known period in the Lucan area that saw the vengeance of the Black Donnellys.

CHAPTER TWO

The Black Donnellys Ride Again

And so the tale began to spread,
That turned the bravest hearts to lead:
Were the Black Donnellys really dead,
Or did they ride again?

— Old Song —

Having witnessed that strangest of funeral services, it was a dazed congregation that left St. Patrick's Church a mile from Lucan, on the afternoon of February 6, 1880. Husky farmers in homespun garments, along with their work-weary wives, were walking towards the roadway and awaiting sleighs and cutters, most of them in an awe-like silence, and for a good reason. They had just attended a church service which even now, though four-score years have passed, is still discussed in the Lucan district. One which seemingly marked the end of an era; the climax of the thirty-three-year-old Donnelly feud.

At the church service the remains of five butchered humans had reposed in two caskets, and the parish priests, the Reverend Father Connolly, had halted during his sermon, unable to continue, and flung himself, sobbing loudly, across the altar.

Of course, even before the mass on that day, a startling story had spread throughout the district like wildfire; one which brought varied fears and emotions to its inhabitants, practically all of whom were either Irish born or direct descendants of sons of the shamrock. It was a story that told of the Donnelly wake, held the previous night at the O'Connor farmhouse, and what had occurred there shortly before five on that very morning. The tale had it that a few hours earlier — soon after midnight — a series of wails and sobs, drawn-out and eerie, floated from a distant, snow-covered field and had been heard by most of those assembled at the farmhouse for the wake.

All who heard the blood-chilling wails agreed that "they sounded like the cryin' of a banshee." Several hours passed, then around 5 a.m., with the first ghostly glow of pre-dawn light beginning to filter through the winter blackness, from out of the bitter cold came a clatter of galloping hoofs, and the following moment, into the O'Connor farmhouse —

"Stepped a masked woman!" declared old Mrs. Dan Flynn, who had been born "just a spit" from the River Shannon more than seven decades earlier. She was to relate the story many times during the remaining six years of her life.

"Sure, an' and 'tis I who will never forget it," she would say when sitting before her kitchen stove and feeling the glow of a hot toddy. "It was just before dawn, and most of the men at the wake were dozin', when the door was flung open and in she walked with the bearin' of a queen — a tall and slender woman, masked, wearing a black cloak that fell to her ankles and her long nails sparkled like jewels in the lamplight. She paid no attention to me or the other women, who were too surprised to speak and just gaped at her; instead, she walked across the room, stood lookin' down at the two caskets for several minutes, and twice I heard her sob. Finally she turned and we all heard: 'They will be avenged — the Donnellys will be avenged, even though blood flows and men die for that victory!'

"Then she laughed a laugh that sent goose pimples runnin' down me spine; that wild laugh which seemed to tear from her heart and rose up like notes on a flute. The next minute she was gone. I hurried to the doorway, saw her run to the road, fling herself on a coal-black horse and thunder away with the speed of the wind. Me poor knees were knockin'; I still bless Mollie Casey for that little nip she so thoughtfully stole from a jug and gave to me."

Although it had happened less than seven hours before the funeral services for the murdered Donnellys, most of the rural parishioners that day, even those living on remote sideroads, had heard the story of the masked woman at the wake long before they reached the church. The tale had a marked effect on the congregation and the same thought was in their minds. Nearly all of them had known the havoc and terror of the thirty-three-year-old Donnelly feud, were heartily fed up with it and glad to be rid of it; and now, just when it appeared to be over, came the story which predicted that more violence and bloodshed were on the way.

Oh, blessed St. Patrick, what was to come next?

As the parishioners left the church, most of them gathered together in pairs or in small groups, as was customary, for brief greetings and discussions on general topics. And believe you me, there was plenty to talk about on that day; material for enough yarns and story-swapping to last for the next three generations. For the once isolated and almost unheard of Lucan area had become nationally known as headlines in leading newspapers throughout Canada made the outside world conscious of the barbarism that had been going on in that district for so long.

Then there was that other matter which caused so much concern and comment among the local inhabitants — the matter of so many strange faces that had been present for the mass that day. This in itself was a wonder of wonders, since visitors to the district were as rare as tickets to heaven. For years, in fact, many families, terrorized by the Donnellys and thinking that they might be next in line, had picked up stakes and left the district, leaving deserted farms behind them, and, in several cases, the very cattle in the fields. Seldom, if ever, did anyone go to Lucan for a pleasure trip, and in the surrounding villages the phrase was commonplace that, "Lucan is a damn good place to stay away from."

Why, even today, you only have to read a history of the district to learn that Lucan was once known as "the wildest spot in Canada."

Yes, visitors were certainly scarce, but on the day of the Donnelly funeral there were a number of them, most of them detectives and Government investigators who had been dispatched there when the appalling massacre became known. Present also were a number of Johnny-on-the-spot reporters, representing leading Canadian papers from as far away as three hundred miles. The grim tragedy and the years of terror that had preceded it promised to be a whale of a story, the only one of its kind in Canadian history and a yarn that could be carried for weeks.

Even America's notorious Hatfield-McCoy fracas or the crimes of the most brutal outlaws and killers of the old West seem like the capers of mischievous little boys when compared to the Donnellys.

As the congregation continued to leave the church at the conclusion of the funeral service, ten or so men gathered beside the gateway leading to the road. They were joined by another man, a stern-featured, swarthy and powerfully-built bruiser of thirty or so, who had the habit of frequently throwing quick glances over his shoulder, as though expecting some lurking enemy to pounce upon him from the rear. It was tall and broad-shouldered Dan Larkin, whose past left much to be desired. A brawler, trouble-maker, liar and souse, who would steal anything that wasn't nailed down, just about sums him up.

Employed on the farm of Cyrus Robbin, the wealthiest man in the district, it was common knowledge that Dan Larkin had been one of the ringleaders of the mob that massacred the Donnellys, though he had yet to be arrested and taken into custody. As he walked up to the gathering, one of the men was telling of the woman who had come to the wake prophesying bloodshed to come. Larkin gave a snort of scorn and snapped, "Wiping out those Donnelly bastards was a killin' well planned, well done and needed. You all know it; I'll horsewhip the man who says different. And now there is a story making the rounds about some fool plannin' to avenge 'em." He pushed back his hat, revealed part of his thick black hair and warned, "Well just let someone try doin' anything about the Donnelly murders, and he'll find he's on a one-way ticket to hell!"

There was a short silence; the others knew that Dan Larkin, a veritable demon when aroused, usually made it a point to lash out with his big fists at the first one who disagreed with him. Undeniably fearless as well as brawny, Larkin had been beaten only once in more than a hundred rough-and-tumble scraps. His one defeat was at the hands of Tom Donnelly who, come to think of it, had beaten him not once but twice on the two occasions when the men had clashed. Tough as he was, Larkin had been no match for Tom Donnelly, but then, no man in the district ever had been.

"The way I heard the story," spoke one of the men at the gateway, "it was a woman who made the threat. A woman who walked into the O'Connor house during the wake, and she wore a black cloak and a mask, so no one knows who she was. Now the question is, who was she?"

"'Tis meself who thinks that the whole story is crazy," spoke another. "Like as not, the whiskey jug was passed too many times during the wake, then someone dreamed up the wild tale, told it to the others and they believed it."

Larkin was skeptical. "Maybe so but I doubt it." he replied and throwing one of his quick glances over his shoulder, went on, "However, I'm tellin' you one thing. What was done to those mad dogs, bloody as it was, was all for the best. Now it's over and that's the way it stays, which is as it should be." His voice rose. "And if any woman comes around here and tries to change things, I will, regardless of her sex, give the meddlin' bitch a kick in the tail that will make her teeth rattle!"

One of the men asked: "Don't you think you'd better make sure you have the right woman, Dan, before you start doin' any kickin'?" The speaker was one Mike Foley.

Eyes hard, Larkin glared at him before saying, "Why the hell is it, Foley that you always worry about things that don't mean a damn?" He went on, "Of course I'll make sure I have the right woman, and when I have finished with her, you can be certain that she will stay in line for the rest of her life — be content to mind her kids, do her washin' and milk the cows as women should. We're not havin' any old hen come in here and try to run things for us. Runnin' things is a man's job."

Then his eyes fell on his employer, the portly Mr. Cyrus Robbin, who was walking towards him, en route from the church to the roadway and his waiting horses. Cyrus Robbin — there was about three hundred pounds of him and he was known locally as "the Squire" — advanced in his usual way, apparently rolling rather than walking, with head held high and eyes half-closed, as though oblivious of the mere mortals around him. But he did pay Dan Larkin's salary; the latter realized it, knew which side his bread was buttered on, and, so he hurried forward to meet him.

The two got into the cutter and, with Larkin driving, sped away, pulled by a prize-winning team of bays, while snow-clusters flew from the horses hoofs and sleighbells jingled.

Among the last to leave the church that day was club-footed William Donnelly, accompanied by his brother Patrick and pretty sister Jennie. Jennie, married and living in the town of St. Thomas, had journeyed to Lucan immediately on hearing of the terrible deaths of her parents and brothers; she was staying at the home of William, four miles from the charred and ugly embers that had once been the family homestead.

As fate would have it, Patrick Donnelly had gone to the village of Thorold, eighty miles away, only two days before the massacre and so escaped the slaughter he otherwise would have known.

William Donnelly, with his brother and sister — as well as his wife, the former Nora Kennedy — had reached the roadway and the waiting horses; in fact they were about to climb aboard the bobsleigh that would take them to William's home, when the first in a series of weird and violent incidents occurred, which were to have a drastic aftermath. An incident which in itself was a quiet and seemingly trivial one, and yet!

As William Donnelly was about to get up on his bobsleigh, a feminine figure left the stream of parishioners passing through the gateway and glided forward — a woman dressed in a winter coat and a heavy black veil that concealed her features. Apparently no one had noticed her, and, least of all, William Donnelly, but for a fleeting instant she was directly behind him, and unnoticed, dropped an envelope into his overcoat pocket. The next moment William had seated himself on the bobsleigh, grasped the reins, shouted to his horses and was driving up the snow-packed highway that was the Roman Line. Behind him, the veiled woman watched his departure before making her way to a nearby cutter.

Yes, in itself it appeared a trivial incident and hardly seems worth the mention, but believe me when I tell you that it was the beginning, the making of the first link in a chain of strange events that was to bring about the startling story that followed. For that same night William Donnelly discovered the envelope which had been dropped into his pocket, as well as the letter it contained. Utterly mystified as to where it had come from — and that went double in spades for his brother Pat — the two read the surprising information the letter contained. Pat Donnelly turned to the other, "But I don't understand," he exclaimed. "It just don't make sense to me. Who is the Midnight Lady and what does she intend to do? In fact, what's it all about?"

"I wish I knew."

"Haven't you any idea?"

William Donnelly made no immediate answer. Instead he frowned in concentration, then, lighting his pipe, sent several smoke-rings ceilingward which rose slowly like lazy ghosts. Finally he again perused the letter, only this time he read it aloud:

"To the Donnelly Brothers:

"Be not discouraged, for vengeance will come as surely as the dawn follows the darkness. Vengeance for you, vengeance for myself, and one which must be brought about though the heavens fall. Therefore, heed well the following:

"None of you remaining Donnelly brothers are to take any steps to seek vengeance till you hear from me again. To do so would jeopardize victory, for there is so much about the massacre of your parents and brothers that you are unaware of, and which even I, at present, cannot fully tell you. For the time being I can only say that the real instigator of the Donnelly massacre is still at large, with his true identity unknown. James Carroll, John Purtell and the four others who have been arrested, suspected of being the ringleaders of the mob were actually only hirelings and dupes — just tools in the hands of a clever fiend, whose lying tongue and false promises actually caused the great tragedy. I will never rest till that man has been brought to justice.

"It may take many days, probably many months and even years, but I shall find him.

"Meanwhile, keep courage till you hear from me

again. And be assured that the day will finally come when you can help me punish the scoundrel who caused the massacre of your parents and brothers, and gain a well earned victory. The hour will come when we will gallop side by side through the night, while once more throughout the countryside the words will be heard: The Black Donnellys Ride Again!

—*The Midnight Lady*"

CHAPTER THREE

Kill Every Damn One of Them

"Go forward," Carroll told the mob,
"And slaughter, slash and slay.
Kill every Donnelly bastard,
Let no one get away."
          — Old Song —

At this point in his story, the old man in the graveyard a mile from Lucan, paused and gave a wan smile to the young American couple who sat before him, so engrossed in his tale and oblivious to all else, the young couple who had journeyed so far to visit the area that had once known the scourge of the Black Donnellys. And now, less than four paces from them, rose the high tombstone that marked the final resting place of that feared family. Then the old man continued:

Well, in order that you may fully understand the almost unbelievable story that followed the Donnelly massacre, it might be best if I were to first speak briefly of the terrible feud itself. As you probably know, it is said to have started away back in 1847, when Jim Donnelly and his wife, fresh from the ould sod, first arrived in Lucan with their two small sons, James Jr.

and William. However, there are certain stories occasionally heard around here which tell that the Donnelly feud actually began in Ireland nearly a century earlier; that it was but continued in Canada by certain families from old Erin who had settled in this practically all-Irish district.

Whether this is true or not will probably never be known, but of one thing we can be certain. On a May day in 1847, Jim Donnelly, along with his wife and two children, drove into the Lucan area — his worldly possessions piled high on the wagon behind which trailed two tethered cows — and he settled on a hundred-acre farm some five miles from Lucan. Trouble started almost immediately.

Now it is not my purpose to either defend or defame Jim Donnelly. I merely wish to state facts as only I know them to be, and in all truth it must be admitted that Jim Donnelly could never be called a lovable character. He was mean, he was vicious, he was a born troublemaker and hated peace. His wife, big, brawny and grim-featured Johannah, had three mottoes that she taught her sons. They were: "Hit first and talk later." "Never forgive your enemies and make no friends." And there was that third bit of advice which she repeated with monotonous regularity: "Always remember and never forget, that when in a rough-and-tumble fight, be sure to get in the first blow — either a hard smash to the jaw or a swift kick to the —!"

Yes, at best she was but a savage old woman with sadistic traits, the kind of unkempt and aged crone who enjoys being in the sick room while the patient dies, who loves to attend funerals while making a pretense at comforting a bereaved family or cheerfully assists in the amputation of an arm or leg. Stories tell that Johannah was the primary cause of the Donnelly feud, and as they grew older, her seven husky sons obeyed her every command. To them she could do no wrong. Any neighbouring farmer who did anything, factual or fancied, that displeased her, was certain to receive a dreaded midnight visit from her wild brood which always resulted in violence and bloodshed.

And it is a matter of record that after her husband murdered John Farrell, old Johannah would tell her sons that she could never look upon them with true motherly pride, "till each of you, like your good father, has killed at least one man."

Back in those distant days when Jim Donnelly first arrived in this district, government land grants were easily obtained, but with practically all of Canada to choose from, Donnelly made it a point to settle on a hundred acres of privately owned land — Lot 18 on the sixth concession of Biddulph Township.

When he heard that an uninvited tenant had taken possession of his acres, the owner of the land rode over, but Jim Donnelly gave him a dreadful beating, threw the man off his own property and threatened him with death if he ever returned.

Strange as it may seem, the landowner made no attempt to regain his property. "I prefer to stay alive" was his explanation, "and somehow, when you look into that Jim Donnelly's eyes, you see the devil and hear the sound of shovels diggin' your grave."

So Jim Donnelly stayed on the land and finished building his cabin. His wife Johannah, as good as any man in lifting a log, even though pregnant, was his only help.

His home built, Jim Donnelly was ready to start breaking ground. For this he needed a plough, stump-pullers and other necessary farm implements. Just how he got them is still a matter of speculation, for it is know that he had little money when he arrived in Lucan. However, common gossip in the area had it that, "farming equipment, strangely disappearing at night from farms out on the Roman Line, always has the damnedest habit of turning up at the Donnelly place. If anything is missing from your farm, just go over to Jim Donnelly's place and you will see it. But try getting it back again and he will kill you."

As mentioned, when they arrived in the Lucan district, Jim and Johannah Donnelly were accompanied by their two small sons, five-year-old James Jr., and two-year-old William, who had been born with a club foot. Four months after settling on the stolen land, on September 16, 1847, Johannah gave birth to her third son, John.

It was handsome John Donnelly, believe it or not, who long after he had been murdered and buried, was the principal reason which brought about the vengeance of the Black Donnellys!

During the eight years following his arrival in the Lucan district, Jim Donnelly whipped the wilderness to a standstill and created a rich, self-sufficient farm. Johannah, on her part, presented him with four more sons, named in order of birth, Patrick, Michael, Robert and Thomas. Johannah's last child was a daughter, Jennie. She was to become the belle of the district. The mother was as fiercely protective of her children as a she-wolf with cubs.

The first eight years of Jim Donnelly's residence in Biddulph Township were marked only with petty quarrels with his neighbors, but his name gradually became an unpopular one. "The Black Donnellys" moniker was to come later. Of course nearly every Saturday night Donnelly rode into Lucan for a drop of spirits at one of its bars and there were occasional fist fights with one of its citizens. Johannah agreed with her husband that a man needs a certain amount of relaxation. At the bars, Donnelly usually had to drink alone and was inevitably the object of hostile glances. Those around him had not forgotten how he obtained his land; also the name Donnelly was now connected with nearly every theft that occurred in the district.

Then in 1855 John Farrell came into the picture and dark clouds began to gather, with murder in the offing.

John Farrell, a husky, fearless Irishman and former blacksmith, bought the acres adjoining the Donnelly farm. Hard feelings soon developed between the two families. It was Farrell who accused Jim Donnelly and his young sons of thievery, of arson and the poisoning of his cattle, as well as just about every other crime under the sun. And it was John Farrell who, on one occasion when telling a group of villagers that some-one had taken a potshot at him from the darkness, said "Of course it was either Jim Donnelly or one of those wild hellions of his. They're as black in sin as their father!"

That is how they got the title, "The Black Donnellys."

Two years passed, with hatred between Donnelly and Farrell increasing. Then, in May 1857, the two met at a logging bee where they got into a drunken brawl. Jim Donnelly killed John Farrell with an iron bar. As Farrell fell to the ground, Donnelly, fighting himself free of the farmers around him, fled back to his home, and for the next two years hid himself in the thick bush at the far end of his farm while the fruitless search continued for him. He burrowed in the hay of his barn during the long winter months, and lived in the woods till the snows came again, but by the spring of 1859 Jim Donnelly had had enough of hiding. One day he walked into Lucan and surrendered.

As John Farrell had been murdered in Huron County's Stephen Township, Jim Donnelly was tried at the Huron Assizes. The trial attracted considerable attention, for although Donnelly himself was not too well known in the Huron district at that time, his name was, as well as the manner in which he had evaded capture. People wanted to see the man who had out-witted the law for more than a year and "worked his fields with his sons, dressed in a woman's clothes." He pleaded self-defence, but there had been more than a score of witnesses to the murder. He was sentenced to be hanged. That night Lucan buzzed with the news, "They're going to hang Jim Donnelly."

But they never did. The verdict was changed to seven years' imprisonment.

Before he was taken away to serve his sentence, he was allowed to speak with his wife. "I'll be gone seven years," he told her, "but I'll be back. Never forget that and never let my boys forget it. I'll be back. And when I return —." He broke off in the middle of the sentence, and the eyes of Jim and Johannah Donnelly met. A few minutes later he was on his way to prison.

The next seven years were marked with countless brawls and violent escapades of the seven growing Donnelly boys against practically everyone in the surrounding district.

True, with their father in jail, the boys were frequently the butt of cruel remarks with regard to the cause of his absence, but as they grew older they were able to avenge all insults with their fists. The Donnellys were not gunfighters. They had a strange aversion to firearms and regarded them as "weapons of the weak, fit only for cowards," but without exception all seven Donnelly boys, as well as their father, were veritable terrors, wild men, in fist and club battles. Detective Hugh McKinnon, former Chief of Police of Belleville, Ontario, once wrote, "When fighting, the Donnellys became howling maniacs, resembling nothing human. It was frightening to watch them as they would snarl, claw and bite with the fury of wild beasts at bay. Each of the Donnelly boys was a match for three average men."

On one occasion, three of the Donnellys put eleven thieving gypsies to flight. Another time, old Jim and his seven wild sons made John Flannigan and seventeen other Lucanites take to their heels. It was said of Tom Donnelly that "he could knock down men as fast as you could set them up before him," and I have personally seen Tom beat five husky farmers into unconsciousness with his big fists.

In the spring of 1863, four years after Jim Donnelly had been sent to prison, numerous petty thefts were reported in the Lucan area. Farmers complained of harness and farm implements disappearing from sheds and barns; village storekeepers told of locked doors being forced open, of looted money boxes and stolen merchandise. There were several cases of village topers, when well-oiled and making their unsteady way homeward, being strong-armed by masked young hoodlums, beaten unconscious and robbed.

All the thefts and attacks, rightly or wrongly, were attributed to the sons of Jim Donnelly, although no formal charges were brought against them. Eventually most of the neighbors would flee at the very sight of their approach, and a wave of fear gradually spread over the countryside — for the seven Donnelly boys were growing up.

Finally, a farmer named Bob McLean and a victim of several thefts, went to the Lucan constable and brought charges against the Donnellys. But it availed him nothing as the charges were denied. The following week Bob McLean's barn went up in flames; the next week it was his house. A few days later, four of this cattle were poisoned and three of his horses were found with their throats cut.

Yes, the Donnelly boys were growing up.

In the fall of 1886, having completed his seven years' prison sentence, Jim Donnelly returned to his family. Now a veritable reign of terror began in the Lucan area and Biddulph Township. For Donnelly had not forgotten past grievances.

One who had witnessed the murder of John Farrell and testified against Jim Donnelly at the latter's trial was a farmer named Haskett. Around midnight, on the very day Jim Donnelly returned to his family, several masked riders rode up to Haskett's barn, yelling like wild Indians, and threw burning faggots into the hay-loft before riding away, while the terrorized Haskett remained within the house. "Despite the masks, I knew who they were. They were the Black Donnellys and they would have killed me if I had stuck my nose out the doorway."

When the vandals rode off, Haskett was able to save his horses but the barn burned to ashes.

For several years after Jim Donnelly returned to his family, he and his sons continued to terrorize the

Biddulph district. There were numerous street brawls
and sideroad gang fights, all of which were won by the
Donnellys. There were several other cases of poisoned
cattle and arson; all of them were rumored as being
the handiwork of the bad boys of Biddulph Township.
But by this time, so great was the dread of them, no
one in the area would dare press charges against the
Donnellys for fear of reprisals. There were a number of
families, grown weary of constant fear, who moved
out of the district.

An example of how the entire district cringed
before the Black Donnellys, can be shown in the case
of Joseph Ryan, a farmer. Ryan, long a victim of Donnelly
abuses, was beaten to a pulp one night by Tom
Donnelly and robbed of eighty dollars. Desperate, Ryan
finally went to the authorities in Lucan to seek help,
and was told, "If the Black Donnellys are against you,
all Biddulph Township can't help you."

Nor were the enforcers of the law safe from old Jim
and his wild brood. At least seven Lucan constables
were given beatings, some of them fearful ones. One
of their victims eventually lost his sight. In fact, in time
the position of a Lucan constable became about as safe
as a pork chop with a hungry lion.

No one suffered more at Donnelly hands than one
Joseph Casswell. There came the summer when
Casswell was unable to get thrashers to help him with
his harvest. Knowing of the Donnellys' hatred for
Casswell, no one would help him in the fields, fearing
dire consequences. Faced with ruin if he could not get
his harvest in, Casswell finally went to the parish priest,
asking if he would intercede for him with the Donnellys.
The good man agreed and asked Jim Donnelly to
allow the thrashers to come in and help Casswell. After

a few minutes' silence, Donnelly's answer was that he would think the matter over and mail his reply.

A few days later the priest received the letter that contained the one word, "No!"

But there is no need to go on and give a lengthy description of the feud itself; you say you have read the book, *The Black Donnellys,* so you know all about it. Suffice to say, and make no mistake about it, for many years Jim Donnelly and his seven wild sons terrorized the Lucan district.

Pretty Jennie Donnelly was married when she was nineteen — that would be back in 1875 — and settled in her husband's home town of St. Thomas, where she raised a family and lived a long and happy life. She and her husband were well respected and numbered among the town's leading citizens. Never was the finger of scorn ever pointed at Jennie.

But how different it was in the case of her parents and brothers! As the years went by, they became more violent and their outrages more outrageous. Their neighbors quailed before them. All the Donnellys, with the exception of Patrick, stood before a judge at one time or other, several of them served prison terms and, in the year 1876, the Donnelly family faced thirteen different criminal charges — charges of arson, highway robbery, poisoning, brawling, drunkenness and wanton destruction.

The passing years brought death to several Donnellys. Some months after robbing a post office, James Donnelly Jr. died of pneumonia in May 1877. Mike Donnelly was murdered by a knife thrust in his back on Christmas Eve in 1879. Finally, fed up with terror, the inhabitants of the Lucan district staged the showdown. The butchery.

Shortly after one a.m., in the cold black morning of February 4, 1880, a mob of thirty men, said to be led by Constable James Carroll of Lucan, broke into the Donnelly farmhouse, and, with cries of "Kill every damn one of them," slaughtered four of the Donnellys — old Jim, his wife, his son, Tom, and his young niece Bridget. They then walked the three miles to the home of William Donnelly, with every intention of killing him too. But fate intervened.

John Donnelly was staying at the home of his brother, and around three a.m. that morning, answering a knock on the door, John opened it to be torn almost to pieces by three shotguns that blasted out simultaneously — shots that were actually meant for his brother William. Later, six men — James Carroll, John Purtell, Martin McLaughlin, John Kennedy and James and Thomas Ryder — were brought to trial and acquitted. The popular expression in Lucan at the time was, "Anyone who killed a Black Donnelly deserves a medal and a special seat in heaven."

So seemingly ended that terrible feud, with the Donnellys beaten and vanquished. A year passed, then strange things began to happen. The terrible story begins in the darkness just before dawn — and far out on the Roman Line!

CHAPTER FOUR

The Midnight Lady

Mounted on a wild devil-horse,
She galloped from the bog;
That masked and black-haired beauty,
Who rode through mist and fog.
— Old Song —

Late on the night of February 3, 1881, Pat and Robert
Donnelly sat with their brother William in the latter's
small farmhouse, some seven miles from the village of
Lucan. Present also was William's wife Nora, who was
telling the others, "I know what you're thinking — the
three of you. You've been thinking it for the last hour.
Maybe longer. That's why you're so quiet."

Handsome Robert Donnelly, a strapping six-footer,
looked at his sister-in-law with a faint smile at the cor-
ners of his mouth. "Have you become a mind-reader,
Nora?" he asked and added: "Well, go on; tell us what
is worrying us."

"It isn't difficult, Bob," was her answer. 'Sure, when
you all sit around the kitchen table, keep staring at the
candle flames without a word being spoken for twenty
minutes, while the hands of the clock on the wall tell
it will soon be midnight, what else could any of you be

37

thinking of but one thing and —"

"Yes," broke in William Donnelly and he nodded to his wife. "We all sit here, knowing that in a few minutes it will be midnight, and February the third will become February the fourth, which will mean it was exactly one year ago —"

"When five of us were murdered by a mob of killers who were never punished," put in Pat Donnelly.

"Men who turn to laugh and sneer at us today," declared his brother Robert. "Nothing can make us forget that. Nothing ever will."

William's wife sighed and shook her head. Formerly Nora Kennedy, she was the sister of one of the six men who had been charged with being the ringleaders in the Donnelly massacre. She well realized that neither her husband nor his two brothers — the surviving Donnellys — could ever forget the past. For that matter, she knew they would never be allowed to forget it. They were the Black Donnellys, and as far as the surrounding countryside was concerned, a thousand years of punishment and repentance could not change that. It was just one of the many crosses that she had to bear in this life.

And all of them because she was the wife of a Black Donnelly. Once a carefree, happy girl — though a rather plain-featured one — she had fallen in love with William Donnelly while still in her teens.

For months they had met secretly. When she finally told her parents of her intentions to marry him, they had stared at her in horrified silence. "I would rather see you dead and in your grave than married to a Donnelly," had been the reply of her mother, while the opinion of her father was even more direct and to the point. He had ordered her out of the house; her brothers and sisters were forbidden even to speak to her again, and former friends and companions made it a point to snub her and show their scorn.

Her married life could hardly have been described as the proverbial bed of roses. It was true that in every way William had been the perfect husband, but to the surrounding countryside he was still a Donnelly, "a mad dog that ought to be destroyed." She was regarded as little better than a whore.

"A penny for your thoughts, Nora," she suddenly heard.

It was her husband and she sensed that he knew what she had been thinking. Diplomatic wife that she was, however, she knew better than to reveal her thoughts and suggested that she make a pot of tea, adding, "By the way, have any of you three come up with a new clue as to the identity of the Midnight Lady, or why she keeps sending us money?"

That name, "the Midnight Lady," had become a symbol of mystery in the Donnelly household. A year earlier, you will remember, William Donnelly had received her first letter, instructing him and his brothers to have courage, but to do nothing in the way of retaliation or vengeance till she appeared among them. Then, a series of letters had followed at monthly intervals, each containing five twenty-dollar bills — and a hundred dollars a month was not hay to any Canadian farmer back in the eighteen eighties. With it, William Donnelly and his wife had been able to live in comfort. Every letter contained a brief message:

"Keep your courage up. The day will come when I will make myself known to you, and the Donnellys will ride again while their enemies flee before them.
                                    —*The Midnight Lady.*"

The last letter — received only two weeks earlier — had held a different message. It informed William Donnelly to get in touch with his two brothers, who had been employed in London, seventeen miles away. It also instructed that the two brothers were to give up their jobs and return to William's abode, "for the hour is fast drawing near when you three brothers and I will strike the first blow for Donnelly vengeance." Pat and Robert had done as requested, though they were as mystified as William by the whole business. It was Pat Donnelly who answered his sister-in-law's question with:

"No, Nora, the three of us are as puzzled as ever as to the identity or true intentions of the one we have yet to lay eyes on."

"She has laid eyes on us," spoke up club-footed William. "Remember when I found the first letter, that day we returned from the funeral. I'm sure it was she who dropped it into my coat pocket when I wasn't looking."

Robert Donnelly, seated at the table and smoking his pipe, sent a smoke-ring ceilingward, observed it, then reminded them, "I've said this a hundred times before, but I'm saying it again. Why would anyone want to help us? No one but a fool does anything without a reason, and in these parts to help a Donnelly is considered a mighty serious offence."

"Quite true, Bob," was William's answer. "But before going into that, the first thing to find out — and it's what we have been trying to find out for a year — is the true identify of the one who calls herself the Midnight Lady."

Pat Donnelly chuckled. "I am sure of one thing," he pointed out. "And that is, that the Midnight Lady is not a native of these parts. You can bet your last dollar on that and I'll tell you why. Show me anyone around here who can keep sending letters with a hundred dollars in them. Or, for that matter, name me one person in Biddulph Township who would like to see the feud resumed or be with us if we rode again."

Then he asked, "And how about you Nora? You're a woman. I've heard they're gifted with strange powers in regard to such matters. What do you think about it all, and are my brothers and I a pack of fools to sit around this farmhouse day after day, waiting for someone we have never met and for a future we can't imagine?"

Nora Donnelly set cups, saucers and a teapot upon the table. She watched her husband pour tea for all of them before she slowly answered, "I don't know. I only wish I could give some good advice, but with things as they are, I honestly don't know what to say."

"Well I do," spoke up Robert Donnelly. "For myself I'm getting mighty fed up with all this mystery and suspense. It strikes me as being some kind of a game of cat-and-mouse. I'm beginning to think I was out of my head to throw in my job in London and come back here. What can it gain me? For that matter, what can it gain any of us? After all, what happened is done and over. Our parents and brothers are dead and there is nothing we can do about it. I'm for grabbing the morning train and returning to London to forget the past and leave the dead rest in peace."

William Donnelly, seated at the kitchen table and with teacup in hand, eyed his brother in mild surprise. Then quietly he remarked: "I never thought I would hear you speak like that, Bob."

"I speak only words of truth," was the reply. "We

can't change the past or bring back the dead, so what would be the use of starting up the feud again? I say forget the past. In fact, I'll say more than that, and add that it might not be a bad idea if we all cleared out of these parts forever and went so damn far away it would take a thousand dollars in one cent stamps to mail us back."

"And let our enemies have the last laugh on us?" asked Pat Donnelly.

"And let our enemies have the last laugh on us," answered Robert with finality in his voice.

A silence of some minutes followed, while the clock on the kitchen wall ticked off the seconds.

The words of Robert Donnelly had come as a surprise to his brothers, but neither of them attempted to continue the discussion and tension was in the air. Instead, the eyes of the three men went again to the flames of the candles on the kitchen table, and each seemed occupied with his own thoughts. Outside, a winter wind was wailing around the house, sending snow flurries hurrying across the windows and over the roof.

Finally Nora Donnelly broke the silence with, "Perhaps it would be best if all of us got into our warm beds, instead of just sitting here — waiting for nothing."

"But we are waiting for something," spoke up William, and again his eyes went to the clock. "We are waiting till three more minutes have passed, till tomorrow becomes today and the date of February 4, 1881 — the first anniversary of the massacre of the Donnellys."

His eyes went to his brothers. "Reflect on that, both of you," he added. "Just about this time, one year ago, our parents and brothers were alive and sleeping in their beds, while that damn gang of killers that butchered them were gathering at the Swamp Schoolhouse to receive their final instructions from that devil of a Carroll."

He leaned forward. "Yes, think about it — particularly you, Bob. Think about it real hard, think about it some more, then decide if you want to forget all about it or not. And, above all, while you're doing your thinking, don't forget to give lots of thought to what those killers did to Mother."

"Don't, William," broke in his wife. "You brothers must never quarrel or find fault with each other. There are only three of you left now. Just the three of you and there must be no hard feelings between you."

Her voice trailed off as she suddenly tensed. The next minute they all knew the reason for her silence, for simultaneously they heard it — the din of galloping hoofs that were ever coming closer. Always closer. Startled, the four exchanged glances.

What could it mean and who could it be at such an hour? There was little likelihood that it was a friend, and highly improbable that a lone enemy would advance upon them in such a manner. The oncoming rider was almost at the house when, as one, the lot of them hurried to the door and flung it open — just in time to see a horse and rider sail over the nearby roadway fence with the ease of a leaf in the wind. The next moment, directly before the door and not six paces from them, the horse was pulled to a sharp halt that flung it on its haunches as snow swirled around it. Then the rider, a masked woman wearing a long black cloak, dismounted, faced them, and they all heard her soft and musical voice, "At long last we meet and there is much that must be done. You three, of course, are the surviving Donnelly brothers and I, I am the Midnight Lady!"

In the kitchen, the clock on the wall began to strike the midnight hour!

CHAPTER FIVE

And Horses Won't Pass
the Donnelly Farm

For the midnight hour brings alarm,
And horses won't pass the Donnelly farm.
Stay off that road or you'll come to harm,
Out on the Roman Line.

— Old Song —

In the golden glow of light that poured from the kitchen doorway on that long-ago night, the Midnight Lady stood before the three surprised Donnelly brothers. Overhead the stars were gleaming.

"Do give me your attention," were her next words, "for something of immediate importance has arisen — something we can turn to advantage against our enemies, to terrorize them — and though the night is as the blackness of the tomb, the Donnellys must ride again. Immediately!"

The brothers gaped at her before William exclaimed: "Ride again? You say we must ride again — and immediately?" Then, at her nod: "But where to?" he asked. "And in the name of sanity — why?"

"I realize that it does come as a great surprise, William Donnelly," came her reply. "Yet if we all go into the kitchen, I can give you ample reasons for such drastic action. But there will be little time to ponder my words; we must ride in a matter of minutes."

In the kitchen, more candles were hurriedly lit and in their glow the Donnellys were able to observe their visitor.

Tall and slender, she wore tight-clinging riding breeches, apparel most unusual for a Canadian woman of eighty years ago. A dark, heavy, waistcoat-style jacket — waist-length — protected her from the cold night, as did her cloak and gloves. Jet black curly hair tumbled to her shoulders; a wide lace mask concealed her eyes and forehead. Her teeth were white and even, and though she spoke in flawless English, the Donnelly brothers detected what they thought to be a slight Spanish accent in her musical voice.

William Donnelly spoke: "My brothers and I have been looking forward to this visit. There is much we want to know."

"With the foremost questions being, who are you, why do you want to help us and why have you been sending us so much money?" asked Robert.

"No one ever helps a Donnelly," informed his brother Pat.

She regarded them for a moment before answering: "Perhaps no one had a reason such as mine for wanting to help the Donnellys, though I cannot tell you what it is, at least for the present."

Then she went on: "As for the money, please speak no more about it, since I intend to keep sending it to you as it means so little to me. Believe me when I say I have much more than I can ever hope to use; in fact, I doubt if the united wealth of the ten foremost families in this district would represent even a fourth of my personal fortune. So let us say no more about money.

"To be sure," went on the Midnight Lady, "it is only natural that you brothers should be suspicious of me, though my only intentions are to help you and to correct a terrible wrong. But as I said, my reason for doing so must remain a secret, at least till vengeance has been ours. But when that day comes — ." She paused, then added, "Yes, when that day comes I will tell you why I seek vengeance with you. And why I ride with you."

William Donnelly looked around the kitchen in a puzzled, helpless manner before he exclaimed:

"But what can I do, what can my brothers do or what can you do to gain vengeance? Why, only yesterday, in the biggest farce in Canadian history, the men who perpetrated the Donnelly massacre were pronounced not guilty and freed!"

All of them realized the truth of William Donnelly's words.

As it had happened, soon after the massacre and acting on bits of information that reached them, the authorities had arrested six men — James Carroll, John Kennedy, Martin McLaughlin, John Purtell and James and Thomas Ryder — and charged them with being ringleaders of the mob. They were brought to trial in London in the fall of 1880, but the jury failed to agree and a second trial was ordered. It began in the last week of January 1881, attracted international attention and ended on February 2, 1881, when the jury filed back into the courtroom with the announcement of "Not guilty!"

The cheers of the spectators rang out in deafening volleys. It was common knowledge that any other verdict would have resulted in chaos. A popular expression of the time was "A jury that would hang the men that killed the Donnellys, should themselves be hung!"

The following day, James Carroll, along with Martin McLaughlin, John Kennedy, John Purtell and James and Thomas Ryder, returned to Lucan in triumph and were greeted in the manner of homecoming heroes. The town band met them and blared sour notes, while the mayor gave a speech of welcome and the populace struggled to shake their hands. A reception was held in their honor at the Central hotel, and later that night a dance was given and joy and festivities reigned in Lucan. The six released men were acclaimed as "the redeemers of the community."

William Donnelly went on with: "At this very moment they are dancing in Lucan, cheering and celebrating the release of the six men who led the mob that murdered my people."

"And it's all legal, do you hear that — it's all legal!" said Robert. "Yes, by God, it's permitted by the law, murderers have been set free and we can't do a damn thing about it." Then he exclaimed, "The sons of bitches!"

The Midnight Lady shook her head. "How wrong you are, Robert Donnelly, oh how very wrong you are," was her answer. "Of course there is something we can do about it, there is something we should do about it and there is something we will do about it."

"Yes, and what is that?" asked Pat. "Do you expect us three Donnellys to ride up to the Central Hotel and charge in on the crown that is there, while we give loud war cries, curse them to hell and swing our clubs?"

The Midnight Lady stamped her foot. It was dramatic and frightening.

"I expect you to use your head Patrick Donnelly and to employ your God-given brains," came her sharp reply before she turned to the others.

"Now hear me. You, too, Nora Donnelly, so you may remember and repeat my words from time to time to these three wild men when they are apt to forget them and resort to force."

The wife of William Donnelly nodded. "I am listening," was her reply.

"First, you must all know of the chief weapon we will employ in the months to follow. It is superstition. Yes, that is it — superstition. There will be no more street brawls, jaw-breaking or gang wars. No more mutilated horses, burning barns and poisoned cattle. All that is in the past and we will let it remain there. My campaign calls for entirely different methods."

"But we were often lied about," broke in William. "We did not do half the things that our enemies said we did."

"Lots of crimes that occurred around here were blamed on us by the very people who did them," spoke Robert Donnelly.

"I know that," was her answer. "Yes, I know you were not guilty of many of the charges that were laid against you, and your very innocence will be of great help in the coming days. But violence will not be necessary. We are going to go much deeper than that; we will play upon the fears your enemies have for the strange and unnatural."

Her words certainly came as a surprise to the others, evident by the startled glances that passed between them. They did not entirely comprehend the words of their beautiful visitor and after a pause, Nora Donnelly admitted it.

"I'm afraid we do not understand you," she said.

The Midnight Lady gave a little laugh. "You soon

will," was her reply before she asked: "Now tell me, William Donnelly, and be honest in your answer. Yes, tell me truthfully, do you believe in banshees, leprechauns or the wee folks?"

"Does he what?" exclaimed William Donnelly's wife.

"Huh? Do I believe in —?" William broke off in the middle of his sentence as his jaw dropped.

"Of course you do," went on the other. "Like so many other Irish settlers around here, you believe in or at least you are not sure that they do not exist, and for that matter who can honestly say whether they do or not? Remember, only a fool laughs at something he does not understand."

"You are quite right, young lady" spoke up Pat Donnelly. "I for one believe in them, and if you could have heard some of the stories my good father used to tell of the strange goings-on he saw with his own eyes when he was a boy in Ireland, you yourself might well believe in the wee folks."

Pat Donnelly went on. "Why I recall a story my father told us a score of times and I never knew him to lie. Well one day when a lad in his early teens, he rowed across the lake beside the farm where he lived to a small island to pick berries. Finally, tired, he lay down on the side of a hill to rest, when suddenly and right before him, up out of the ground popped a little old man with long whiskers whose head would hardly come to your knee and — "

"The little old man was dressed all in green, he wore a tall hat, he took out a clay pipe and started to smoke it," interrupted the Midnight Lady. "This went on for several minutes. Finally the little man happened to turn around, saw your father and the next instant he vanished." Then she asked:

"Now isn't that the story you were going to tell me?"

It was, and the Donnelly brothers realized as much, as they had heard it many times in their youth; but it had been a tale told strictly for the family — one not meant to be repeated beyond the Donnelly walls. Just how the masked woman before them knew of the story they had no way of telling, but the next moment they heard her say:

"Someday I will tell you how I happened to hear that story, but for the present it has proved my point — that there are many Irish people who believe in the strange and unusual. I intend to play upon those fears in the days to come. Such being the case, let me continue.

"You were right, William Donnelly," she went on, "when you said that at this moment, in Lucan, they are celebrating the release of the six men who led the mob that murdered your parents. Yes, that is quite true indeed they are, but what you do not know about is a newly hatched plan."

"What plan?" asked William.

"Shortly after one a.m. — about an hour from now — several men who were in the mob and are now making merry in the Lucan hotel plan to ride past the charred remains of your farmhouse and drink a toast to their successful raid of a year ago!"

It was quite true. The man who had first thought of the brutal idea was John Turtell, a half-wit and sadist, one of the mob members on that night of horror who had helped to slash and butcher young Bridget Donnelly.

When the Midnight Lady came out with her startling information, there were gasps of surprise from the Donnellys before Robert exclaimed:

"They plan to ride out to the old farmhouse and drink a toast to their success?"

"But that's inhuman — vile, rotten and inhuman! That's a desecration!" shouted Robert. "Not only do those devils murder our parents and brothers and get away with it, now they are going to celebrate the occasion, to gloat and laugh over their victory, and at our helplessness to do anything about it."

"Like hell they will!"

It was William Donnelly. He leaped forward with raised fists and flashing eyes. "No one is going to laugh at our dead as long as we are able to swing a club!" He shouted. "Let them try and we'll take them apart — piece by piece!"

He turned to Pat and Robert, "Come on," he ordered. "Get your horses, let's start ridin'; we'll gallop over to the old farm, meet that bunch of murderers when they get there, beat hell out of them, maybe kill a few, then — "

"Right!" spoke his brothers in unision.

"Yes, be sure and do that, start killing your enemies then terminate your days by dangling at the end of a rope!" snapped the Midnight Lady. "What ails you three? Have you lost any wits you ever possessed?"

Once more she stamped her foot in an irate manner. Her gaze went to Pat Donnelly, then to Robert, before it returned to William, while the clock on the wall continued to tick away the seconds. She pointed to it:

"See," she observed, "time continues to carry on, at a period when every minute is so important to us, yet you three do nothing but form a wild, impossible plan, which, even if successful from your point of view can mean nothing but your own ruination! Where are your brains?"

Her words caused the Donnelly brothers to halt, then Nora, William's wife, spoke sharply: "I sometimes doubt if they have any brains, young lady." Then, addressing the brothers "If you three hot-headed fools will listen to her, I'm sure you will find logic in her words and common sense in anything she asks you to do."

"And it must be done quickly," spoke the Midnight Lady. "As I once wrote you, William Donnelly — and I trust you remember it — James Carroll and the five others who were charged with being the ringleaders of the mob though guilty of the charge, were actually only dupes and hirelings of the one who caused the deaths of your parents and brothers — the cruel mastermind behind it all."

She went on: "That man — that monster of murder — walks the streets of Lucan today. Yes, the one who was principally responsible for the Donnelly massacre is regarded as a leading citizen, a gentleman without fault, and his true guilt is known only to two others. That will all change, I promise. The hour will come when I will reveal him and his crime to the countryside. Then he shall be punished and the vengeance of the Donnellys will be realized. But for the time being we must forget about him. Right now there is another and immediate matter before us."

Her eyes went to Pat Donnelly as one hand gestured to the door.

"Out there, in the saddle-bag on my horse, you will find three costumes — three tight-fitting painted garments that you brothers are to don hurriedly, after which you will get your horses and ride with me. But there is not time for explanations. Too many minutes have already been wasted, Patrick Donnelly, but if you

really want to accomplish something and strike the
first blow that will eventually bring around the downfall of your enemies, ask no questions. Just do what I
say — and quickly!"

"Yes boys, do what she says," put in Nora Donnelly.
"For my woman's heart tells me that we can trust her,
also that she knows what she is doing. Yes, do what
the Midnight Lady says!"

The clock on the wall struck twelve-thirty.

It was a half-hour later, at one o'clock in the morning of February 4, 1881 — when seven horsemen drew
up near the charred and snow-covered ruins that had
once been the Donnelly farmhouse. A full moon was
sailing across the sky.

Laughing, boisterous and well filled with the juice
of joy, the horsemen, all of them former members of
the mob, were returning to the scene of their bloody
crime to drink a toast to their victory. A short while
earlier they had left the celebration party in the village
of Lucan after announcing their intentions. Some of the
villagers thought the idea was quite clever, and this
went double in spades for John Purtell, one of the riders. When a quarter of a mile away from the Donnelly
farm, the seven came to a long-deserted, crumbling
farmhouse. Purtell drew in his horse and motioned the
others to do the same.

"Look at it, boys. There it is — the old Farrell place.
Still standing after all this time. Poor John Farrell. He
was murdered over twenty years ago by that damn Jim
Donnelly. Let's guzzle a drink to Farrell's memory."

The others drew in their mounts; whisky bottles
were produced and sampled. Around them winter
winds whistled over snow-covered fields; ahead and

behind them were long stretches of the road they were travelling — the notorious Roman Line, of which it had been said: "The farther down the road you go the tougher the folks get, and the Donnellys live in the last house!"

There was some truth in these words. Living along the Roman Line were husky Irish immigrants with their equally husky offspring, for ninety-five percent of the Lucan area was inhabited by sons and daughters of the ould sod, along with their descendants. It was the best place in the world for a quarrelsome and trouble-loving man to go. He would quickly be obliged. He could get all the fights he wanted with no questions asked. And believe me, those tough, rough Irishmen knew how to fight — with nothing barred!

Gun-fighters? Well — no. Along with the Donnellys, the other inhabitants of that wild district knew little or nothing about firearms, and generally regarded guns as "weapons of the weak — fit only for cowards." They were strictly fist and club fighters, with the Donnelly boys head and shoulders above the rest. They were the undisputed champions. Hardy men quailed before them and on one occasion, in a fist and club battle — the story can still be heard around here — five of the Donnelly boys put thirteen thieving gypsies to flight in a gory battle.

There was also the time when old Jim Donnelly and his seven handsome sons whipped the living daylights out of John Flannigan and sixteen other Lucanites in a fist and club battle. It ended with the Flannigan horde in wild retreat, with each man looking as though he had passed through the meat grinder.

But in the early hours of that cold February, when the seven horsemen rode down the Roman Line in rowdy triumph, the Donnellys had been vanquished for exactly one year, their power to terrorize and instill fear into the hearts of others was over — vanished, gone forever. John Purtell, whisky bottle in a gloved hand, made a remark to that effect, which was answered by loud laughs and chuckles, and one of the men called out:

"By the horns of old Nick, we have nothing more to fear from the Donnellys — now or ever." He added: "Nothing more to fear, that is, unless the bastards can come back from the pits of hell and haunt us!"

Amid loud guffaws, another recalled: "Remember what old Johannah said as we were clubbing the old sow to death? She shouted that we would all know a violent death. Also, that she and the others would come back from the grave and ride again!"

More drunken laughter followed.

By this time the horsemen were less than fifty yards from the path that led to the blackened ruins of what had once been the Donnelly farmhouse, behind which was the dark outline of a large and still-standing barn. Though bitterly cold, it was a clear night bathed in the glow of a full moon and agleam with stars. The riders continued to advance at a slow canter; night winds whipped up and sent miniature snow-clouds swirling around them. Then, less than ten yards away from the gateway, it happened!

Yes, it happened. And by the Beard of Buddah, how it happened!

Suddenly, and certainly very unexpectedly, from out of the darkness of the roadway ahead came the din of galloping hoofs. And as the entire seven drew reins and gaped in surprise, from the gloom came a masked and slender figure on a coal-black horse, whose long

cloak streamed out full length in the breeze. It was the
Midnight Lady, of course. To be sure it was the
Midnight Lady — ah, but that was only half of it. For
she was not alone that night; no, most certainly she
was not alone! Right behind her, each urging a horse
forward at hell-bent-for-leather speed, as blood-chilling wails stabbed the night —.

"Came three mounted skeletons!" John Purtell was
to tell some skeptical listeners in Lucan a short while
later, while his lips trembled and his features were still
a ghastly white.

"It's the truth, so help me!" Purtell shouted, as the
grins of his listeners showed their disbelief. "I tell you
that I and the six men who were with me saw them —
we saw them as plain as the nose on your face — we
saw them because we were there, they were there and
that's what they were — three full-grown skeletons on
horseback who rode behind a masked woman in a
long black cloak that whipped out in the wind as she
galloped forward! Yes, and they charged straight down
towards us, the whole lot of them. The skeletons gave
out with screeches like lost souls in hell, while the full
moon beamed on their bleached bones and their fiery-
eyed horses snorted!"

There was a stunned silence for several minutes,
then one of the listeners asked: "Well, what did you
do?"

Purtell glared at the speaker before he roared:

"Do? You ask what did we do?" John Purtell took a
deep breath, brought a fist down hard on the table
beside him and bellowed: "What the hell do you think
we did, you half-wit? We did what anyone else would
have done; we did what you would have done if some
howling skeletons were to come charging down upon

you. We wheeled our horses, didn't bother to look back, rode like hell and got out of there as though the devil himself was on our heels."

He turned to those who had ridden with him to the Donnelly farmhouse and asked: "Ain't that right boys?"

Noticeably awed and frightened, they all nodded.

Of course no one in Lucan believed either Purtell or the other six who told the same story. Now by that I mean, at first nobody believed them. They attributed the seemingly impossible yarn as the result of too much giggle water and imagination. But as the days passed and the seven men continued to tell the same story over and over — "and they were willing to swear on the holy book as they did so" — there were those throughout the district who began to wonder if there might not be a bit of truth in the story, fantastic as it seemed. And, bear in mind, that eighty years ago, most of the Irish inhabitants of the Lucan territory were great believers in the wee folks, banshees and the supernatural.

So it was that at around the time when spring was well under way, a story began to spread that the ruins around the old Donnelly place were haunted.

Nor was that all. There were certain folks who would relate that during the dark hours before dawn, strange lights of many colors flashed on and off above the fields surrounding the farm, while wild screams and terrible laughter could occasionally be heard. Screams and laughter that did not come from the throats of the living. Others swore that the dead Donnellys continued to gallop up and down the Roman Line once the sun went down. One Jack Keefe, a one-armed farmer, souse, thief, and a notorious liar, told that he, too, had seen the three skeletons and the

Midnight Lady on several occasions as they galloped their horses across broad fields in the moonlight.

Finally came the story that on the anniversary of the massacre, wailing ghosts were abroad and it was impossible to get a horse to go past the old Donnelly place after midnight. This story continued to be told even with the passing of the years. Strange as it may seem, it can still be heard in the Lucan district even to this day.

And there are many who say — including myself — that the story is true!

CHAPTER SIX

The Donnellys Have
Come Back from the Grave

"Days passed and then a tale was told,
That sickened folks with fright:
'The dead Donnellys ride the Roman Line,
In the blackness of the night.' "
— Old Song —

At this point in his story, the old man in the graveyard paused, then chuckled.

"Of course," he said to the young American couple, "you have already guessed the identity of the three skeletons who rode with the Midnight Lady on that night and other nights to follow. To be sure, it was the three surviving Donnelly brothers — William, Robert and Pat — and they wore the costumes their leader had given them. The black tights and hoods, skillfully adorned with phosphorescent paint, realistically resembled the skull and bones of a skeleton, especially in the darkness."

Surprise sprang to the features of Ann and Don Graham, then the latter exclaimed: "Well I'll be damned! So that's how the Midnight Lady did it and was able to scare the pants off Purtell and the six others. She certainly had all the answers!"

61

"But where was she able to get such tights — tights that resembled skeletons?" broke in blonde Ann Graham. "Eighty years ago there would have been no place around here where she could have got them."

The old man gave a quiet laugh before he answered: "You are a very observant young woman to be sure, though in this case you have erred."

Ann wanted to know just how she had erred.

"Well, you see, the Midnight Lady had planned her campaign thoroughly, even long before she began it. Along with many other schemes, she had devised a plan that would enable the three Donnelly brothers to resemble skeletons when they rode with her, and from a costume firm in New York had purchased the grotesque-looking tights she had brought with her to Lucan."

"And no one ever suspected the truth?" asked Ann Graham.

"To the best of my knowledge, no one was ever absolutely sure," came the answer. "For a number of weeks after their first appearance at the Donnelly farm, the three brothers — attired in their skeleton costumes — continued to gallop behind the Midnight Lady up and down the long Roman Line in the hours of darkness, while Pat, Robert and William made the night air tremble with their wild shouts and war cries. There were housewives who would tell of being awakened by the sound of thundering hoofs and yells. They would hurry to the bedroom window to catch glimpses of that grim foursome."

Don Graham spoke up: "But what did it accomplish? How could all that ghost business hope to help the Midnight Lady or the Donnelly brothers? What could it gain them?"

Around them the last fading glow of sundown was like a golden spotlight from space. Soon would come the shades of eventide, then the glow would disappear in the gradually darkening hues of night. Birds still chirped in the surrounding trees, squirrels chattered and scolded, while on all sides tombstones, many erected more than a century ago, stood out as silent and tireless sentries. In the distance they heard the faint barking of a farm dog.

At Don Graham's question, the old man stared at him in surprise before answering:

"You ask what did it gain the Midnight Lady and the Donnelly brothers to go galloping up and down the Roman Line at midnight?"

"I did. What was their reason for doing so?"

"Why the reason strikes me as being quite apparent, young man," came the answer. "It was to instill fear and awe in the hearts of the surrounding countryside. Fear, awe — and yes — to bewilder folks as well. That was most important — very important. The Midnight Lady knew it was absolutely necessary that the inhabitants of the Lucan district be kept in a state of unrest and fear, before she would be able to continue with her plan to destroy the enemies of the Donnellys."

Don and Ann Graham exchanged glances, then the latter asked: "Well, was she able to do it — did she destroy the enemies of the Donnellys? And if so, how was it accomplished?"

The old man raised a hand in protest. "Please, please — not so fast. The Midnight Lady accomplished a great deal, and those who knew her will never forget her; but I cannot tell you all that she did in a matter of twenty words or so, for it is a startling story;

a story so fantastic as to be almost brain-reeling. But it is true, it did happen and it all happened right where you are at this moment — with the climax less than a mile from here, when a great monster met an incredible death and his blood turned the grass to a sticky crimson!"

Needless to say — the old man went on after a pause — for a number of days after their appearance, the entire Lucan area spoke of little else than the masked woman and the three skeletons.

"Yells and wails came from their bony mouths as they charged towards us," John Purtell would inform his listeners as he told and retold his story. "I tell you I knew I had heard them before or at least something damn near like them. In fact, the more I think of it, the more I believe that they were exactly like the hellish war-cries and shrieks that the Donnelly boys used to give out with when they were galloping over the countryside burning barns, poisoning cattle, cutting tongues out of horses, beating up folks and raising hell in general."

When someone said that it might have been the skeletons of some of the murdered Donnellys that he had beheld, Purtell would invariably answer:

"Knowing that damn Donnelly bunch like I did, it wouldn't surprise me a bit if they continued to ride on and on, even if you killed them a thousand times. There was always something weird and unearthly about the Donnellys. Something inhuman about the bastards!"

February faded into March, March to April and the deep snows in and around the Lucan district finally melted. They left behind ponds and miniature brooks that sparkled and gurgled on and across broad fields, green and fresh in the first warm sun-rays of spring. Next came the buds on the trees as nature gave promise of an early summer, but local gossip was only of the four midnight riders.

Then came May 1881, and the spine-tingling experience that caused most of the inhabitants of Biddulph Township to become weak with horror and shock when they heard of it.

To begin with, as everyone knew who had heard the narrators tell it, the story had to be true. There could be no possibility of it being but the figment of an overwrought imagination, a deliberate lie or a hoax. Oh no, it had to be true, for it was told by old Mr. and Mrs. Michael Ryan, who were, and had been for a long time, regarded as just about the most honest and most truthful couple in the Lucan district. They lived in a small house on a few acres a mile or so from the village and had never missed a Sunday appearance in church in more than seventy years. Both in their late seventies and none too-well fixed with this world's goods, their honesty was beyond question.

The story, which was to spread throughout the district like wildfire by nightfall, got under way about ten thirty on a Saturday morning, when Mr. and Mrs. Ryan drove their buggy into Lucan at — what was for them — breakneck speed, and it was evident that the old couple were in a state of shock and excitement. They babbled a few words to nearby loiterers as their buggy halted in the centre of the village; seconds later said loiterers were shouting to all the others within sight. A short while later, in Hanley's General Store — and surrounded by a score of villagers — the old couple were fairly shouting out the fantastic news:

They had just seen and talked with four of the murdered Donnellys — old Jim Donnelly, his wife Johannah and two of their sons, Tom and John. Yes, and they not only talked with them; more than that, the four Donnellys had been in their small home for more than an hour, and had actually sat down and had breakfast with them.

"And it's the truth," Mrs. Ryan exclaimed to her listeners. "You have all known my husband and me for years; you should, for we were one of the first pair in this district and have lived less than a mile from the village for more than forty years. All right, now tell me, in all that time have any one of you ever heard either my husband or me tell a lie or spread a false rumor?" she demanded.

Of course not, the others assured her. She and her husband had always been a highly respected couple, their word was unquestioned. With her husband standing beside her, white-haired, leaning heavily on his cane and nodding silent affirmations from time to time, she continued.

Well, it seemed that Mrs. Ryan and her husband had slept a bit late on that particular morning; it had been nearly seven when they arose. Then, a bit before eight, with the wood in the stove crackling, the tea-kettle singing and eggs and bacon frying, there had come a loud knocking on the kitchen door. She had gone to open it, and there, standing before them, friendly and smiling, were the four Donnellys who had been clubbed to death, burned, then buried, more than fifteen months earlier. They were all dressed in their Sunday-best, and a lily was in the hand of each!

Not only that, as they opened the door, old Johannah Donnelly had greeted:

"Tis the top of the mornin' to you, dear Mrs. Ryan; also to your grand, good man, and may your garden yield a fine crop of praties come the fall, while your cows give only crame so thick a duck could walk on it." She explained their presence with: "My husband and I, along with our sons Tom and John, left our graves early this mornin' and started walkin' across the green fields, when we sighted your house and decided to drop in for a wee chat."

Then she had turned to her son Tom and reminded: "You know, Tom darlin', as I have told you several times, it was dear Mrs. Ryan who helped to bring you into the world."

Then, according to Mrs. Ryan and her husband — whose honesty, as mentioned, was beyond question — the four Donnellys had walked into the kitchen, where they drew up chairs and made themselves at home — as Johannah explained — "like the dear friends we are." Of course the hearts of old Mrs. Ryan and her spouse were beating like trip-hammers, eyes wide, jaws dropped and throats paralyzed, unable to make any utterance. But their four visitors seemed unaware of their terror. They chatted gaily on, speaking of local events and apparently quite interested in the prospective church social that had been planned for the following week.

At no time did they make the slightest mention of the massacre or how they had been able to return from the dead, though old Jim Donnelly had finally hinted that the lot of them "were a mite bit hungry since food is pretty scarce when you're lying in a moldy grave!"

So Mrs. Ryan had hurriedly fried more bacon and eggs, as well as some cold potatoes, which her visitors ate with gusto. When Tom Donnelly finally pushed his chair from the table, he grunted happily, "By Judas, I needed that."

"But what was far more terrible than anything else," Mrs. Ryan had cried as she told the story, "was the awful odor that seemed to drift from them to us, a strong musty smell like that of the grave! And there was that worm on Johannah's cheek that seemed to be burrowing its way deeper and deeper into her flesh; but she paid no attention to it, didn't seem to even know that it was there. Oh, it was awful to watch. Me knees grew weak; I kept thinkin' I was going to faint."

"By all the snakes St. Patrick drove out of Ireland, I though I would go out of my mind, so I did," put in her husband. "Neither me nor me old woman could say a word or do other than gape at them, for our tongues were frozen with shock, our minds dulled; but the Donnellys didn't notice our silence; at least it didn't seem that they did. They just talked on and on —mostly to themselves!"

Hands shaking, halting frequently in her narration and looking at her husband for numerous confirmations, old Mrs. Ryan went on with her story. According to her, the four Donnellys remained in the kitchen for the better part of an hour. Finally saying they had to be on their way, as there were urgent matters that needed their attention, the visitors rose, made their way to the kitchen doorway and passed through the opening. Their former carefree manner had suddenly gone; they had become grim-faced and quiet — exactly as the Ryans had known them in bygone years. Now they were the Black Donnellys!

Once outside the house, the four walked in silence to the Ryan barn, then followed on down the narrow pathway that led around it and on towards the fields. It seemed evident that they had some weighty matter on their minds, wished to ponder it and say no more; but as Johannah Donnelly followed the others and just before she disappeared behind the barn, she suddenly turned and called back to the elderly Ryans who were framed in the kitchen doorway.

"I've a message you can tell the Lucan folks," she shouted in her harsh, masculine-like voice. "Tell them you have seen us, that we have indeed returned from the grave, for the Black Donnellys have unbelievable powers that can recall us from the dead. Our enemies will soon learn that!"

She went on. "Tell the countryside that during the months to come, the Lucan district will know a reign of terror such as it never knew even during the most violent days of the feud. It will be a period of stark hell and madness. Tell folks that we four will make weekly Saturday night raids — and promptly at midnight upon the homes of various members of the mob that massacred us. One by one we will visit them all and demand a frightful vengeance — a hideous payment that will make your blood turn to ice when you hear of it! And we can and will do it, for we are the Black Donnellys!"

Her voice rose higher — and louder. She raised two clenched fists and shook them at the sky, her stout, muscular body shaking with rage.

"A week from tonight," she shrieked, "we make our first raid and it will be on the home of Dan Dunn, the black devil that chopped off my husband's head. Ah, but we'll get him! The following week we'll deal with Barney Harrigan, for he was the one who heated the poker that was used on me. Tell those two bastardly blatherskites that there is no way they can escape us

— no way ever — unless they put a hundred miles between them and this district before we visit them, and they must never return.

"Tell folks that every Saturday night at midnight — and one by one — we will deal with every damn member of the mob that murdered us!"

Then, according to the narrator, old Johannah gave out a long, loud and dismal Donnelly war-cry that made the air tremble, before she turned to follow the others and disappear behind the barn. The elderly Ryans — a pair in a trance-like state — continued to stand in the kitchen doorway, wide-eyed and speechless. They saw the four Donnellys trudging northward like macabre scarecrows as they cut across the field behind a barn.

The Ryans watched until the foursome became mere specks that finally disappeared into the horizon.

"And it's the truth, every word I have told you is the truth," Mrs. Ryan was finally concluding in Hanley's general store amid gulps and frightened sobs, while her flabbergasted listeners — there were about thirty of them when she finished her story — looked on in speechless wonder and silence.

"Yes, the Donnellys have come back from the grave!" she wailed, "and you'll all soon learn how true my words are, come next Saturday night — at midnight — for that is when they will ride in on the home of Dan Dunn. Oh, God help us; God help us all, for it means the old scourge has returned, once again there will be nights of fire, blood and terror!"

"Only this time we won't be dealing with ordinary people of flesh and blood that can be overpowered by superior numbers, halted and killed," put in her husband. "This time it is different; this time we have to face terrible things of hate and destruction, out to destroy this district, with whom we cannot battle, before whom we are absolutely helpless. This time we must face horrible, vile-smelling things of evil, that leave their dank and moldy graves at midnight, then ride in on us! This time we face the dead Black Donnellys!"

Before nightfall the story had swept over the entire countryside. Terror was abroad!

CHAPTER SEVEN

The Grim Fate of Dan Dunn

They found him in an upstairs room,
He lay half beneath the bed.
Blood flowed around his lifeless form —
In one corner was his head.
— Old Song —

Mr. Cyrus Robbin, the wealthiest man in the Lucan district, rarely permitted himself to become interested in anything that was not beneficial to the three hundred pounds of blubber, broad behind and pot-belly that was his well-fed and cared for self. Despite his money, the old walrus firmly believed that charity should begin at home and stay there. He wouldn't have given a duck a drink if he owned Lake Ontario; he was about as popular as a skunk at a picnic, and he possessed as much of the milk of human kindness as you'd find in a concrete sidewalk.

In brief, Cyrus Robbin loved and helped only Cyrus Robbin. To meet him was to dislike him; to speak to him was to hate him; to know him an hour was to loathe his guts and his belly for carrying them!

However, Cyrus Robbin — known as "the Squire" — could not be classified as small potatoes. On the contrary, around the Lucan district he was the big frog in the pond. He knew it, enjoyed his importance and played it to the hilt. One of the earliest settlers in the territory and son of a wealthy English merchant, at the age of fifty-seven Cyrus Robbin owned a number of the surrounding farms and half the village of Lucan, as well as a prosperous business concern in London. Living in a large white house a mile from Lucan, and a widower for seven years, it had long been whispered among the inhabitants of the district that "poor Mrs. Robbin had welcomed death."

And they might have had something there, as the guy did draw flies.

Around nine p.m. on the same day that the Ryans had driven into Lucan to tell their amazing story, ten men had been sent for and were assembled in the parlor of Cyrus Robbin's home. All of them sons of the soil and dressed in homespuns, most of them worked on the various farms owned by Robbin. They all had one thing in common, along with their red faces and large hands. Every last man had been a member of the mob that massacred the Black Donnellys. None of them were overly endowed with brains; they were accustomed to taking the Squire's orders and letting him do their thinking for them. Not men, only zombies; just sheep following their leader.

Dan Larkin, Robbin's husky farmhand, as well as bodyguard and what have you, was telling the others:

"And that's why you're all here, so sit still, stop askin' questions and wait till the Squire comes in from the barn, where he's lookin' over a new mare he just bought. Like I told the lot of you, he's heard about the damn crazy story that old lady Ryan and her husband are spreadin' around; he thinks it best that we should make plans to do somethin' about it. If we don't, the whole district will be crazy with fear in a week. They'll start to think that there is a ghost a poppin' up behind every tree, and we can't afford to let that happen."

The others nodded and Larkin added: "It could bring in a lot of snoopers askin' questions, and it wouldn't do any of us here much good if the word got out that all of us had had a hand in murderin' those damn Donnellys!"

A brawny and swarthy-faced man in his early thirties, who had a habit of throwing quick glances over his shoulder as though he were expecting an attack from the rear, Don Larkin had been employed by Cyrus Robbin for the past ten years and obeyed his fat boss without question. Larkin had been a conspicuous member of the mob and had personally clubbed young Bridget Donnelly to death and later assisted in the burning of the Donnelly homestead. Undeniably fearless and hard as nails, he was also a brawler with his fists and had a habitual snarl-like tone in his voice.

One of the men spoke up. "Dan I'm worried as hell as are all of us here. Why in the name of the devil can't those Donnelly murders be forgotten, become a thing of the past? After all, it was more than a year ago; there is no reason why it should be brought up again. The dead should be forgotten. I tell you I don't like it. I don't like any part of it — and I'm a bit frightened as well. I'd be a damn liar if I said I wasn't."

The speaker was Dan Dunn, a short, stocky man with a thick, blue-black beard and an enormous chest. He was the same Dan Dunn — according to the story — that the "dead" Donnellys had promised they would deal with first — a week hence and promptly at midnight. And wild and impossible as the story was, Dan

Dunn was plainly worried. He kept wiping his forehead with a dirty blue bandana, his eyes constantly sweeping the room.

His fear amused Dan Larkin, who regarded him with a faint smile. "I can understand why you're frightened Dunn. Yes, it's easy to figger out. Accordin' to the story, the dead Donnellys remember that it was you who axed off old Jim's head." Larkin shrugged. "Well, you never can tell. Maybe they will chop off your head in payment."

"Stop it!"

Dan Dunn waved a hand in an impatient manner. "Don't talk so silly man; don't say things like that. Now who the hell ever heard of folks who could come back from the grave and kill the livin'? It's impossible; it just can't be done."

Larkin was enjoying the other's fear and pressed on. "Well, you never can tell, can you? For that matter, neither can we. It looks like we'll just have to wait till next Saturday night and see what happens to you. As I understand it, the story goes that the dead Donnellys plan to raid your house and do something hellish to you, unless you put a hundred miles between you and Lucan and never return. Of course if you want to stay here and call their bluff, that's up to you."

Further conversation was silenced by the sudden appearance of the Squire.

As usual, Mr. Cyrus Robbin was meticulously dressed in a suit of coal-black, his thick hair combed back in a pompadour. Cyrus Robbin was six feet tall, had an enormous paunch and bushy eyebrows; he was clean-shaven and his shoulders brushed either side of the doorway. He had a habit of carrying his head high, frequently closing his eyes while he talked, and he held his nose in the air as though everything around him stank. Oddly enough, for all his bulk, his voice was unusually soft, almost feminine in tone. Folks who had known him, even for years, never ceased to wonder at that soft voice coming from such a large man.

Immediately on entering the room, Cyrus Robbin spoke to the others clasping his white hands together.

"Good evening gentlemen. I had my man, Dan Larkin, ride over and summon you here, for I understand, due to some wild story told this morning in the village, that a wave of fear is sweeping over the countryside. Of course the story is utter rot, fantastic and impossible, even though it was told by an elderly couple hitherto known for their honesty. So as men of intelligence we must regard it as the prattle of two aged tongues that have strayed from the path of honesty to the field of fiction."

He cleared his throat, said "Ho-humm" then said, "Do I make myself clear?"

The others — practically all of them dependent on him — nodded to their lord and master.

Then Cyrus Robbin explained his plan. He said it was up to the others to keep fear from spreading throughout the township; that the wise thing, the only thing, was to ridicule the story of the Ryans to farmers near and far, saying that it was nothing but the ravings of two aged people more than a mite bit touched in the head. Though he knew that all of them — himself excluded, of course — had participated in the massacre of the Donnellys, he said no one would ever know if they did not show any sign of fear. Nobody could prove anything. They must stand firm, all of them, and dismiss the story with a laugh. They must show no sign of being worried.

"Remember," he reminded, with eyes half closed and leaning forward, "that the wild story might have been told by the Ryans for just one purpose."

He went on. "Who knows? For reasons of their own, someone could have put the Ryans up to tell such a story, wholly to note the reactions of those who heard it, hoping that in some way the unknown slayers of the Donnellys would betray their identity by panic or flight — a story told, shall we say, to create an ever mounting fear in the killers and so flush them out into the open, and cause them to betray themselves.

"You must be aware, once the guilt of any member of the mob that murdered the Donnellys is known, it will be but a matter of hours till he is arrested, and only a short while later until, hoping for clemency, he reveals the names of the others. Needless to say, you realize that such a confession would be ruinous to every one of you here, and could result either in life prison terms or a mass hanging. Therefore, it is my advice that you stick together and do nothing to betray your guilt. That is all. Goodnight, gentlemen."

Like docile sheep they all rose and made for the door, leaving the Squire to himself. None of them, not even Cyrus Robbin, had been aware of the diminutive figure just outside the house, crouched beneath a half-open parlor window, who had heard every word that was spoken. The figure rose and slouched away into the darkness on some mission of its own!

The following Thursday afternoon, William Donnelly drove his buggy into Lucan. He appeared to be in a very jovial mood. As usual, Paddy, his aged crow, sat on his right shoulder.

Paddy was a familiar sight in Lucan and had been

for years. An unusually large bird with as harsh a "caw" as had ever rasped out of any crow, Paddy had been found by William when he was all beak and claws and was giving out with his first faint chirps after falling from his nest. After that one was rarely seen without the other; and around 1881 the then ageing Paddy was still — according to his owner — quite a dancer. The crow had been taught and seemed to enjoy spreading his wings and hopping rapidly up and around on a floor, on a table or bartop, while nearby, William Donnelly would saw out the Devil's Reel on his trusty fiddle, and exclaim, "by the stones of Blarney Castle — what a bird!"

On the day in question William had both Paddy and his fiddle with him.

William Donnelly brought his buggy to a halt in front of the Central Hotel, and, walking with the slight limp caused by his clubfoot and with Paddy clinging tightly to his shoulder, he went inside for a few stiff ones. There, lined up against the bar or sitting in battered chairs around equally battered tables, were fifteen or so farmers, idlers and bar-flies. No matter how late or early the hour, the village bars in that Irish community were rarely empty, as the inhabitants were mighty thirsty souls; while any man who could not down a pint of raw spirits without removing the bottle from his lips was regarded a sissy.

At one time, believe it or not, although the population was less than five hundred, there were nine bars in Lucan. In 1879 in a period of less than thirty days, both McRobert's Old Dominion Hotel and Fitzhenry's Hotel were destroyed by fire. It was the general opinion of the countryside that it just had to be "the work of the Black Donnellys up to their old tricks again!"

When William Donnelly walked into the Central Hotel bar on that long-ago Thursday afternoon, the general conversation died away while all eyes went to him. His presence was something of a surprise, since clubfoot Billy had not been seen in any bar since the massacre of his parents and brothers over a year earlier, and all the inmates in that room of soothing beverages somehow sensed that his being there was a warning of sinister things to come. However, he was smiling broadly as he walked up to the bar and called for a drink of rye. As was the custom, a bottle was pushed forward. William downed his first drink — a generous four-fingers — straight, refilled his glass, then spoke to the bartender, Jack Doyle, in a voice loud enough for the others to hear.

"You can wrap up three quarts of rye, Jack, to take along with me."

"Three quarts? You must intend to have some kind of a party."

"Well, you could say that," was the answer. "You see, my dear mother and father, along with brothers Tom and John will be dropping in to see me Saturday night, and they'll all like a few nips to take the chill out of their bones. They tell me it gets real cold down there in their graves — cold, black and silent."

There were gasps from the listeners. For the next ten seconds you could have heard a pin drop in that barroom. And why not? They have heard it with their own ears, they had distinctly heard every word he said; he was ordering whisky for four people who had been dead for over a year! The bartender, bug-eyed, glared at him, then finally sputtered:

"You — you say you want whisky for your dead parents and brothers; that they are coming to see you?

Is that what you're trying to say?"

"That's what I am saying, Jack," William Donnelly replied, a slight smile on his lips. "From what they've told me, they'll all be pretty busy Saturday night, and I want to warm their bellies for them when they drop in. I understand they also plan to drop in and see Dan Dunn, though I don't expect it will be a very friendly call." He gave a laugh and added:

"You know, Jack, to tell the truth, I don't think Dan Dunn will like that visit at all, at all. Sure an' it's my own opinion, when my folks get through with him, that his own mother wouldn't recognize Dan Dunn. That is, if there will be anything left of him to recognize — which I doubt!"

With that, William Donnelly lifted his refilled glass to his lips, drained it and set it down on the bar. He paid Jack Dolan for the three bottles that were handed to him; he started for the door, when, for the first time, he let his gaze run over the assembly and his eyes came to rest on John Purtell. Again a laugh escaped his lips, but this time it was harsh and mirthless — the terrible and typical Donnelly laugh that foretold of violence to come. He pointed a finger at Purtell, pushed it forward and said:

"Don't worry, John, my people won't forget you; they'll get around to see you in time, just like they'll call on every man who was in the mob that murdered them. One call every Saturday night for the next thirty weeks is their schedule, and you are on the list as sure as the devil's in hell. They told me so!"

William Donnelly turned, walked out of the bar, got in his buggy, wheeled it around and, with his horse at a slow trot, started down the village street towards the Roman Line, a mile away. But that was not all; no, not quite all. Folks who happened to be on the street at the time later told that, as William Donnelly drove out of Lucan, he had his violin to his chin and was loudly playing a rousing rendition of the Devil's Reel while Paddy swayed back and forth on his shoulder, giving out with rasping caws and flapping his wings. It must have been a sight to behold.

By the time Saturday night rolled around, with the promised raid on the home of Dan Dunn but a few hours away, fear and excitement swept the district. Why, even the village bars were practically deserted and most folks stayed indoors, with the big question being — what would happen? Was the story true or was the story false? Many village and farm housewives for miles around spent the hours before midnight on their knees in prayer, as they implored the Almighty to see to it that the dead Donnellys had sense enough to remain in their graves, where all good corpses belonged, and to stay there — permanently!

As for Dan Dunn himself, that stocky gent with the blue-black whiskers, he was rapidly approaching panic as the midnight hour drew nearer. By eleven his jangled nerves had reached such a state, that he felt he had only to cut his suspenders to go straight up!

He was not destined to go without help, however. Others rallied around him; others who, like himself, had been members of the mob. Two days earlier, on the order of Cyrus Robbin, his man, Dan Larkin, had ridden over to Dunn's place to inform him that he would be amply protected on Saturday night.

"You have nothing to worry about, Dunn," Larkin had told him. "Mr. Robbin has arranged for me to have a dozen armed men around your home on Saturday night, just in case that there might be trouble of some kind. Of course none of us believe that wild fairy tale about the dead Donnellys coming back from the grave to get you, but just in case somebody tries to do some funny business, we'll be there to help you. Now get a hold of yourself, man; don't lose your nerve and go to pieces."

So it came about that, shortly after eleven on that Saturday night, twelve men, led by husky Dan Larkin, arrived at the Dunn farmhouse. All of them actually participants in the Donnelly massacre, they surrounded the house at strategic positions, each man armed with a shotgun. Any party who came to the house that night, intent on harming Dunn, was certain to receive a warm reception.

The house was surrounded. Dan Larkin, carrying his shotgun, went inside. He found the black-bearded Dunn, ghastly white, trembling, and on the verge of collapse. The guy had had it. Dunn pointed to the kitchen clock that told the midnight hour was less than twenty minutes off; then he made a shaky way to a chair, flopped down on it and half-sobbed, "Nothing can save me, Larkin. I've been thinking of it for several days and can't take any more. They're coming; I feel it in my bones. They'll be here, just like they said, promptly at midnight and nothing can save me!"

Larkin gave him a look of scorn." Don't be a damn fool, you ninny!" he snapped. "Nothing is going to happen to you. The house is surrounded; no one can get in here. I have eleven armed men outside who'll blast the daylights out of any living human who —."

"But that's it; that's just it. They're not living humans."

"Shut up!" interrupted Larkin. "That story you heard is the blackest of lies; dead men don't leave their graves — Black Donnellys or no Black Donnellys — and you'd know it if you had a brain in your head. Now stop showing that you've a yard-wide yellow streak and try acting like a man. And think, what would Cyrus Robbin say if he saw you behaving this way?"

But the other soon made it plain that the opinion of Cyrus Robbin didn't mean even one good damn to him. "To hell with what Cyrus Robbin would say," shouted Dan Dunn. "Why should I think of him at a time like this? It's my hide, my skin that the Donnellys are after, not his — though we both know if there was any justice in the world, that it would be his and not mine!"

"Yes? What do you mean by that?" demanded Larkin.

Dan Dunn, unmarried and a confirmed woman hater, got to his feet as desperation seized him. A desperation similar to that of a cornered rat, fighting for its life. He pointed an accusing finger at Larkin.

"You know damn well what I mean," he cried. "We both know it was that fat and holy hypocrite, Cyrus Robbin, who was the instigator of it all; who was behind the whole rotten business from start to finish and who brought about the massacre of the Donnellys. I'm sick of keeping it a secret any longer. Why should I?"

"Shut up, Dunn!"

"I won't shut up," screamed Dunn, "and if you and the other fools want to go on kissing his broad behind because he's rich that's up to you. But for me, I'm going to start talking and tell Lucan the real truth about its leading citizen. Then I'll tell the world!"

"I said shut up!"

"And I say I won't! The truth's got to come out! We both know that Cyrus Robbin is the real murderer of the Donnellys. Safe and snug in his big house, he gave the orders and masterminded the massacre! You and I and the others who did it were just a pack of weak, spineless fools — deceived by his lies, filled with whisky and doing his dirty work for him — who slashed, tortured, beat and burned to please Cyrus Robbin. And I'll tell you why!"

Dan Dunn's voice rose to a shriek: "It's because that fat bastard owns practically this entire district and we are his slaves, paper-men without any minds of our own, to do with as he chooses. It's because we are indebted to him; owe him money and back rent, can't do without him and must bow down before him. But I'm through with all that, Larkin; I tell you I'm through with it, for I know a way out! The only way out!"

Dan Dunn wheeled, ran to the nearby stairway and bounded to his bedroom. Surprised, Dan Larkin watched his wild disappearance, shrugged, then turned, walked out into the open and called quietly to one of the men stationed near the doorway:

"Connors, come here."

Connors, shotgun in hand, came forward to ask: "How's Dunn holding up? When we got here he was shaky; a minute ago I heard him shouting like a mad-man."

"The fool has gone crazy with fear, stark crazy," informed Larkin. "Yes, and what's worse, he's threatening to go to Lucan and name the men that murdered the Donnellys. I don't have to tell you what that would mean to you, me and the others."

"But Dunn was with us when we did it. He helped with the killings; it was he who cut off Jim Donnelly's head."

"I know, but he's gone out of his mind, I tell you.

Don't know what he's saying and he's dangerous." answered Larkin. "There is only one thing to do; we'll wait around here till midnight has gone to prove how false the damn story is, then we'll take Dunn to Mr. Robbin, even if we have to tie him up and throw him across a horse to get him there!"

The other agreed. "Of course; we can't let him start shooting off his big mouth to folks. Why if word ever got around that —"

His voice trailed off, at the sudden striking of the kitchen clock announcing midnight. In the quiet of the night, the other men surrounding the house could also hear the clanging. They realized that it was the time limit they had been waiting for. Each passing second heralded the next one; and as they all stood there, silent, tense and listening, there came the final striking of the clock — eight — nine — ten — eleven —

And then, came a loud, sharp sound. It was the blast of a shotgun going off at the exact second the clock struck twelve. All the men recognized it for what it was. There were sharp exclamations of surprise, then with Larkin leading, the lot of them raced into the house, tore across the parlor, up the stairs and into the bedroom of Dan Dunn.

They found him lying on his bedroom floor in a pool of blood, while crimson drops smeared that blue-black beard, stained the walls and ceiling, and smoke still curled from the barrel of his shotgun. His head had been practically blown from his body. Wide-eyed, hearts pounding and speechless, the men stared at the grim tragedy whose cause was so apparent. Crazed with terror as to what might happen to him, as the kitchen clock began striking, Dan Dunn had removed one shoe, placed the barrel of the shotgun into his mouth and with his stockinged toe had pushed the trigger. The sight would have curdled your guts!

But what made the whole damn thing so utterly nightmarish was the fact that murderer Dan Dunn had died exactly at the stroke of twelve — precisely at the very second foretold by the Ryans!

CHAPTER EIGHT

"He Went to Hell in Pieces"

He lashed his horse on fast towards
The crossing in the east.
At the track the train cut him apart,
On his flesh the crows did feast.
— Old Song —

"Barney Harrigan gets it next! The Donnellys said he was number two on their list! God help him, come next Saturday midnight!"

Yes, those were the words that were said a thousand times throughout the Lucan territory during the week following the violent death of Dan Dunn. In the village, on main roads and on lonely sideroads, folk gathered around kitchen tables with the coming of darkness, and in the glow of lamp or candlelight — sometimes speaking in whispers — made grim and terrible prophecies as to the impending fate of Barney Harrigan. Nor was that all; conflicting stories began to be heard about Dan Dunn's death. To be sure, there were many who said that, crazed with fear, he had taken his own life.

Ah, but there were other tales — blood-chilling tales — that he had not committed suicide; that instead

89

— unseen by the men surrounding the house — the four dead Donnellys had floated through the open upstairs bedroom window, and the hand of old Johannah Donnelly had actually pulled the trigger of the shotgun that blew off Dan Dunn's head. Then — according to some of the stories — the triumphant laughter of the Donnellys had rung out, loud and wild — "scaring the pants off the men around the house, though they won't admit it!"

Nor was that all. During that week there were ever increasing rumors of a masked woman on a coal-black horse, whose long cloak whipped out in the wind behind her as she rode up and down the Roman Line in the black of the night. More and more night travelers claimed they had seen her. At times, it was said, she rode alone. Occasionally she was accompanied by three mounted skeletons, who galloped behind her, their terrible howls and wails rising to the stars!

And if all that were not enough, regularly now — every day in fact — William Donnelly would drive the ten long miles from his home to Lucan and back. As his horse went along at a slow trot, William would play the Devil's Reel on his fiddle. He would play it over and over, as black Paddy, clinging to his shoulder, swayed, screeched and flapped his wings. This, the surrounding inhabitants agreed, boded no good. It was a warning; the calm before the storm. A terrible storm of violence and destruction was coming as sure as God made little apples.

It was more than enough for the none too courageous folks; for them caution was the better part of valor, and they didn't want to wait around and find out just what would happen. They decided, to hell with it all. And so, once again — as it happened so frequently during the wild days of the feud — families began to move out of the Lucan district, and once more the words were heard:

"Lucan is a damn good place to stay away from!"

One Friday afternoon Dan Larkin was summoned to the parlor of Cyrus Robbin, and it was evident to the husky Larkin that the Squire was in an ugly mood — he was pacing the floor, hands locked behind him and frowning. He raised his eyes at the entrance of his employee.

"Larkin," he demanded, "where have you been?"

"Why, out in the barn, sir," was the reply. "Out in the barn, bawling hell out of that drunken little Danny Doyle, who'll do anything but work and I still don't know why you hired him. I told him I wanted all the stalls cleaned out and bedded down by noon, and I find the little Irish souse sleeping off a jag in the haymow."

Cyrus Robbin waved an impatient hand. "Forget Danny Doyle. There is a far more important matter that needs immediate attention. Now give me yours."

Gray haired and grizzled, Danny Doyle had long been a familiar figure in the Lucan district. Not quite five-feet tall, weighing no more than a hundred pounds — sopping wet — and well past the sixty mark, old Danny could drink seasoned topers under the table, and for the past six months had been employed as a stable hand on Cyrus Robbin's farm. Before that he had spent most of his time as a souse and barfly in Lucan; but somehow, for all of that — and despite his insatiable thirst — he was a lovable old cuss. Generous, big-hearted and honest as they come, poor Danny was his own worst enemy.

But Cyrus Robbin was not interested in little Danny

that afternoon and said: "Things around here are going from bad to worse. Dan Dunn made a fool of himself, and now I have learned that that imbecile of a Barney Harrigan is rapidly going to pieces — wild eyed, acting crazy. He's even going around shouting out that he is damned; that at midnight tomorrow he will be dead."

Larkin nodded. "Yes, so I've heard. He's a spineless whelp!"

Cyrus Robbin regarded his employee for a minute, then his eyes narrowed. An expression of cunning crossed his features and he asked: "Did it ever occur to you that there is something more than meets the eye behind this wave of terror that is sweeping over the district: stories about the dead Donnellys returning from their graves; wild tales that tell of riding skeletons and a strange masked woman who gallops up and down the Roman Line in the darkness?"

He leaned forward, his so very soft voice becoming almost a whisper. "Yes, Larkin, there is something very strange about it all and I'd like to tell you what I think. Nothing gets by me for very long, and I believe that I have solved the mystery."

"You have?"

"To be sure; it all points to one possible solution. There is a very clever brain behind it all who, for some reason I do not know at this time, is causing those many wild stories to make the rounds and for just one purpose, to bring panic to the thirty men who murdered the Donnellys, to cause them to betray their identity by their own fear, at least some of them, who will then be arrested and in turn name the others who were with them at the massacre."

"Which could result in my arrest as well as all the

others who had a hand in the killings," put in Larkin. Then, at the other's nod, Larkin asked:

"Well, what are you going to do about it? You weren't there the night of the killings, so you have nothing to worry about. It's different with me; I've plenty to worry about if tongues start waggin'. I don't like the idea of ending my days standing at the end of a rope. After all — and don't forget it — we were only following your orders. You know that."

Cyrus Robbin was a master at manufacturing a phony smile, and he did just that as he spoke: "Relax my dear fellow, relax and be calm; have I ever failed you? Of course I intend to take care of everything," he said, "and I will take the first steps tonight. I am going to make a call on that elderly couple, the Ryans, whose blabbering tongues first started that wild story of vengeance from beyond the grave. And remember — that farm they are on — well, they are behind in their payments to me."

He went on to say that that very night he would drive over and call on the Ryans, then demand that they publicly retract their story of having talked with the dead Donnellys. They would be forced to admit that their story was a pack of lies. This, the Squire pointed out, would be of tremendous value in getting folks back to sane thinking and forgetting about dead Donnellys. Once that was done, he would make it a point to have several of his men find and ride down the masked woman who was known as the Midnight Lady. He had a hunch that she might well be the one behind the whole weird business, the instigator of all those crazy stories.

"But all in due course, Larkin; we will take things as they come," he concluded. "First I will ride out to the

Ryans, and if they refuse to publicly retract their story, I will foreclose on them. It is my opinion, and it usually is a correct one, that the threat of their being kicked off the place — and at their age — will more than make them see things my way and do as I tell them."

Larkin understood; his knowing grin was a grimace of evil. "Quite right; I see what you mean, sir."

The other nodded, clapped his fat white hands sharply together and announced: "That will be all, Larkin. Send Danny Doyle into town with the light cart for the poultry feed you need, then at eight sharp tonight have the bays harnessed and before the door."

Larkin withdrew; once again neither he nor Cyrus Robbin had noticed the small figure crouched just outside the window listening to every word. It was Danny Doyle and later that day, when driving towards the village for the poultry supplies, old Danny whipped up the horses and rapidly drove a mile out of his way to deliver a most important message.

Cyrus Robbin was a bewildered man that Friday night as he left the small house of the Michael Ryans and began the three-mile drive back to his own home. It was a few minutes before eleven.

The bewilderment of the massive Mr. Robbin was due to the seemingly almost fantastic prosperity of Mr. and Mrs. Michael Ryan. He had become aware of the fact that dame fortune was indeed smiling on them when he first arrived at their small house and observed it had recently been painted. Met at the door by the Ryans — both dressed in new, expensive and store bought garments — the surprised "Squire" soon discovered that they also possessed a new stove, and had been unpacking several pieces of furniture bought in

London; while a fast harness horse and two cows —
purchased that very day — slept in the barn that
Michael Ryan mentioned he would "soon tear down
and build a new one — yes, and maybe even a new
house."

And then Cyrus Robbin's surprise had changed to
down-right, speechless amazement when six hundred
dollars was placed on the kitchen table; a sum that
cancelled the Ryans' debt to him. Needless to say he
was made to acknowledge the payment in writing
before he received the money.

It was just too much for the Squire — his legs had
gone weak, his head spinned. With a sickly smile he
had accepted the offer of several cups of tea, along with
three large helpings of apple pie; for that big belly of
his could sure stow it away, and, besides, it was free. But
for all his shrewdness and glibness, he had been unable
to worm out even the slightest bit of information as to
how they had acquired their new wealth. The couple
had met his every question with a skillful verbal parry,
and a number of quiet smiles — knowing smiles —
that were most annoying to their guest. When he left
he was none the wiser than he had been on his arrival.
And when he had suggested that their story about the
visit of the dead Donnellys to their home was an
incredible lie, Mrs. Ryan had stated with finality:

"The story is quite true, Mr. Robbin. I have no
doubt that the Donnellys will do exactly what Mrs.
Donnelly promised they would do — raid the home of
and punish every man who was in the mob on the
night of the massacre!"

He left the house, got into his buggy, whipped up
his splendid team of bays and started homeward. It was
then Cyrus Robbin realized, due to his many surprises

and drawn-out snack, that his stay at the Ryan place had been much longer than he had anticipated, and for all the speed of his horses, eleven o'clock found him still two miles from his home. A heavy rain had fallen earlier in the day, a stiff wind was blowing, and black clouds that hid both moon and stars only helped to increase the darkness of the night. A gloomy old night at best, on that lonely side road he had taken as a shortcut, with the golden twinkles from farmhouses few and far between. Too damn far between, thought Cyrus Robbin.

On he drove, but it seemed to Cyrus Robbin that the wind was gradually changing to a series of mournful, drawn-out sobs. It was lonely; a certain tension was in the air and the night was black as pitch. He began to feel uneasy; in fact he began to feel damn uneasy and started to take backward and sideward glances, wishing he had asked Dan Larkin to accompany him. Then, out of the darkness ahead he heard the clatter of oncoming hoofs. Cyrus Robbin pulled hard on the reins; he shouted to his horses and brought them to a stop — just as the oncoming rider came into the glow of the lantern on the seat beside him. A gasp escaped his lips.

It was a masked figure on a coal-black horse; a slender figure whose long cloak swirled in the wind while thick wavy hair tumbled to her shoulders. And somehow he knew her identity! Yes, though he had never seen her before, he intuitively realized that it could be only one person. The strange one who rode the roads in the wee small hours and was known as the Midnight Lady! Then he heard:

"Greetings, Cyrus Robbin, and do come closer, for I have been expecting you, waiting for you. The hour is late — an appropriate time for our meeting — a time when most souls take their flight!"

Never much of a hero, the musical voice caused the enormous Cyrus Robbin to quiver, then to shake. Involuntarily he shook his head as though to clear it, half rose from the buggy seat, then sat down again. His throat was dry, he was unable to find his voice for a minute, finally from his lips came a half-squeaked noise.

"Who — who are you? Yes, and what do — do you want?"

He heard a laugh like the tinkle of distant chimes — far-away, exotic, cool and lovely. Then: "Oh come now, Mr. Robbin; you surely know who I am," came her reply. "Why only this afternoon you were telling that brute of a Larkin how you were going to have some of your men find and ride me down. Remember?"

That was true, but how in the name of Jupiter had she learned that information?

"As to what I want," she went on, "it is to inform you that from now on it will be very dangerous for you to be found on any road in this area, once the sun has gone down. Remember that if you want to keep on living — even for a while!

"You see, Mr. Robbin, gradually my noose is tightening. One by one I intend to punish the thirty men who participated in the Donnelly massacre, and one of them — Dan Dunn — has already paid the price. However, that still leaves twenty-nine to be dealt with; I will take care of them, I promise you; then I am going after the leader — the one responsible for it all, the one whose lying tongue brought about those murders!"

She paused, and as the wind swirled her cloak around her and her mount rose up on its hind legs, eager and impatient to be off, she called out:

"Do I have to tell you who that man is, Mr. Robbin?"

"Then she wheeled that great devil of a black horse and was off like a shot — like an arrow from a bow!" Cyrus Robbin was telling Dan Larkin a short while later. "My God, Larkin — the speed of that horse!" he exclaimed. "Why I have never seen anything like it — I tell you it was fantastic! One minute they were there, the next they had vanished from sight, and I heard hoofs galloping off into the darkness at a speed I would have sworn was impossible! That horse of hers must be half-devil!"

In his parlor, Cyrus Robbin, ghostly white, wiped a palm across his forehead. Fear still shone in his eyes.

"But you say she knew you were planning to have men ride her down and capture her," put in the stalwart Larkin. "That she said she knew you had spoken of doing it this afternoon — which you did. Now what I want to know is, how the hell did she know? I never repeated your words to a soul, and you and I were alone here in the parlor when you said it."

"I don't know, Larkin. I do not know!"

Cyrus Robbin began to pace the floor, all three hundred pounds of him, head low and hands behind him. Beads of perspiration stood out on his forehead. After several minutes he paused, turned and said:

"No, it is beyond me how she knew of my plan and I will probably never know the answer, but I can tell you one thing — we are up against a strange and crafty enemy who, for some reason of her own, has taken up a campaign to bring the murderers of the Donnellys to justice — every last man of them. And I don't have to tell you what that means to you and me. But what can be her purpose? Why does she want to meddle in something that cannot possibly concern her?

Why, Larkin? Why?"

Dan Larkin could only shrug and wonder what would come next. He also realized that Cyrus Robbin was a very worried man. And more than a bit frightened, too!

The following afternoon — Saturday — the sun was starting to lower in the west when Barney Harrigan, a week's growth of whiskers on his usually clean-shaven face, staggered from a Lucan saloon, disheveled, bleary-eyed, loud-voiced and worried. The same Barney Harrigan who, according to certain stories being heard throughout the district, now had less than seven hours between him and a midnight visit from the Black Donnellys!

"And oh, Lord love a duck, 'tis the dead Black Donnellys he will be meetin', so 'tis, so 'tis! THE DEAD BLACK DONNELLYS!"

As Barney Harrigan left that emporium of soothing beverages and made his unsteady way to the street, the bartender turned to the people watching Harrigan's departure and remarked: "Sure an' poor Barney hasn't drawn a sober breath in the last week, but then you can hardly blame him. No one has much stomach to face four ghosts!"

"Shiftless" Jack Quinn, a habitual barfly, petty thief and a figure loathed by most of the villagers, spoke up: "I said it from the first and I'm saying it now. All those yarns about dead Donnellys coming back from the grave and killing the men that killed them are crazy."

"Then if the killers of the Donnellys aren't to be touched, you don't have a thing to worry you, do you, Quinn?!"

Standing at the far end of the bar, the speaker was

little Danny Doyle, who had driven into the village for his usual Saturday afternoon battle with John Barleycorn. Shiftless Jack Quinn, hearing the remark, turned and glared hard at tiny Danny, while others snickered, since it was known that Quinn — for five dollars and two bottles of whiskey — had been a participant in the Donnelly massacre. Shiftless Jack — tall, thin, with rotting teeth, about forty-five and dressed in tattered clothing a self-respecting scarecrow wouldn't be seen in — snapped out:

"Why the hell don't you keep you damn mouth shut, you little souse?"

Danny was grinning at his own words; his grin widened at Quinn's reply and he started to chuckle. "What's the matter Quinn, can't you stand hearing the truth about yourself?" he asked, then added: "And as for calling me a souse, why to match my drinking against your own is like trying to compare the arse end of a lightning-bug to the noonday sun!"

Laughter arose from the other guzzlers. Suddenly loud shouting resounded from the street, which sent them all hurrying through the swinging doors to investigate.

Standing in his buggy in the centre of the street was Barney Harrigan, shouting at the top of his voice. Being Saturday, there were shoppers about who had driven into the village for supplies. They stared in wide-eyed silence. Of course all of them knew of the grim prophecies regarding Harrigan's fate come midnight, and for once he found himself the centre of attention — an eminence you can be damn sure he did not want. As the saloon's inmates piled forth into the street, Harrigan was still standing upright in the buggy. His battered hat hung over one ear, a half-empty whiskey bottle was in one hand, and while a stray mongrel barked loudly in the street, he yelled:

"Go on, go on! Look at me, keep staring at me, you bunch of black-hearted, curious bastards! Yes, go ahead and look! Look your God damn eyes out! Feast your eyes, your bellies and your souls! Glut your very brains — and titter while you do it — on the man you think the Black Donnellys are going to grind to mince-meat come midnight. Sure — sure — stare away; stare till your damn eyes drop out, the lot of you! After all, you're safe — it's just me that's got to die! Your own hides are safe!"

He swept one hand around him in a wild, waving circle. He coughed three times, spat on to the road, then went on: "But you're not looking at a beaten rooster — no, you're not by a damn sight. You're not watching a rooster just standing around the chopping block waiting for the axe to separate his head from his carcass! Not me — no, not me! I'm not givin' up my pelt without a struggle! Not by a damn sight I'm not!"

From the sidewalk, someone called out: "Wheel you buggy westward and go home, Barney. You're drunk!"

Harrigan glared at the speaker with the fury of a maniac bent on murder. "Drunk am I?" he howled. "Yes, I am drunk, but I am also a man of brains, a man of reason and a man of action. And as such, I'm not standing around waiting for the Donnellys to come for me. I'm getting the hell out of this district, I am; out of the country, too — and I'm leaving now! Right now!"

That was it. The next minute Barney Harrigan grabbed the driving reins in his left hand, his whip in the other, and brought the whip down on the glossy rump on his horse in a vicious crack that sent the beast bounding ahead and racing down the street with the speed of a derby winner. Once beyond the village limits, heading eastward, the buggy rumbled at a good clip, since Harrigan's horse was reputed to be one of the fastest in the district. And it was sure forced on to the last bit of its speed that day as the drunken Harrigan, oblivious to all else but flight, kept shouting and lashing at it with his whip in the manner of a frenzied devil.

And that was the last the good folks of Lucan were ever to see of Barney Harrigan. At least, that was the last they were ever to see of him alive; and what some of them did see of him later was anything but pretty. For it seems there was a great metal monster which Barney Harrigan either failed to see or else choose to race against that day — an oncoming engine and a four-car train. Engine and buggy crashed together at the train crossing a mile and a half east of Lucan in a grim race that ended in a dead heat.

Both horse and driver were flung upwards as the buggy burst into a thousand pieces, some of them the size of match sticks. As for Barney Harrigan, it was later said that they didn't have to pick him up! They swept him up!

During the following week, William Donnelly, when driving his buggy from his home to Lucan and back, would frequently pause in his fiddle playing to tell passing folks: "Barney Harrigan, the second victim of Donnelly vengeance, went to hell in pieces!"

Two days after Harrigan's death — the following Monday — it was learned that Shiftless Jack Quinn had left the district for parts unknown, on the previous night. He is said to have died two years later hopelessly insane in a Toronto madhouse, shrieking in his final moments: "I see her; I tell you I can see old Johannah Donnelly now! She's standing right there at the foot of my cot. She's come from the grave, she's all covered with blood; she's beckoning to me and she's laughing! No, don't let her take me! Oh God help me!"

CHAPTER NINE

I'll Brand My Initials on Her Rump

Days passed and then a rumor spread,
That was told in Lucan town.
The Donnelly killers plan to ride,
The Midnight Lady down.
           — Old Song —

Where you are now, Biddulph Township — went on the old man in the graveyard — is a flat, fertile district, ideal for farming; bordered on the east by Perth County, on the west and north by Huron County. Eighteen miles away is London, where in pioneer days unlicensed marriages were performed at crossroads at midnight, with the bride and groom attired only in their nighties.

Following the death of Barney Harrigan, Lucan readied itself for the next tragic happening. "And there will be many of them, I can promise you." warned old Grandma Bell. "Many tragic happenings and much bloodshed!"

That brought a gasp from those who heard the words, and with good reason. Grandma Bell, the last of a small black colony that had settled near Lucan eighty years earlier, had lived through one hundred and four

105

years, and was well known throughout the district for her uncanny powers as a teacup reader. When she made a prophecy folks made it a point to sit up, take notice — and believe. For more than half a century, Grandma Bell had amazed the surrounding inhabitants with the accuracy of her fortune telling, and had been instrumental in the recovery of lost or stolen farm equipment and cattle, as well as in encouraging young couples to venture down the road of matrimony with her promises of a sunny future.

Her predictions always had the damnedest habit of working out exactly as she said they would. That went double in spades for her prophecies.

Of course the old woman's biggest claim to fame — and it was a well authenticated story — was her prediction of the Donnelly massacre to old Jim Donnelly himself — two months before it happened. It happened on a windy night in November 1879, when Jim Donnelly, along with three of his sons, Mike, Tom and John, pulled up their horses before her small log house. The old woman, who later told and retold her story many times, once related it to a reporter. It appeared as an editorial in a London paper in her own words:

"There was blood on the moon that night, and I was sitting right here in the kitchen. It was around nine o'clock when I heard their horses being pulled up before the house. The next moment they came through the door, the four of them, crazy drunk and laughing. I knew Mr. Donnelly and had spoken to him several times in the past. I had seen the others, too, and I knew they were his sons, but I didn't know which was which. Mr. Donnelly said: 'Granny, we want you to tell us our fortunes.' "

"Then he pointed to one of his sons and said, 'This

is Mike.'"

Mike smiled, waved his hat and shouted, 'Hello Granny, I hope my fortune says I'm going to find five barrels of gold!'

The father pointed to another son and said, 'This is John.'

"John was a handsome man, though not as heavy as the others." He smiled and said 'Hello.'"

"The father said, 'And the other one is Tom.'

"I looked twice at Tom. I had heard he was the terrible one who had beat so many men with his big fists. He did not smile, he didn't speak; he just stared at me and his eyes were cold.

"I knew they would not harm me. Mr. Donnelly had always been friendly and smiled when he saw me; yet I did not want to tell them their fortunes. But when he asked me again I made some tea, and after they drank it I saw in the tea leaves what was before them. There was blood on the moon that night and I could see it all plainly.

"Mr. Donnelly asked: 'Well, Granny, what do you see?' And I told him, 'I see death, Mr. Donnelly; death for you, death for your wife and your sons here! I see death for all of you — soon and terrible!'

"They laughed at me; oh, how they shouted and laughed. Mr. Donnelly threw a coin on the table, and said my words were the funniest he had ever heard. Then they all ran out and got on their horses. I could still hear them laughing as they rode up the road. The next I heard of them was when a neighbor ran over to tell me they were all dead! They — Mr. Donnelly, Mrs. Donnelly, John, Tom and Mike — had all been murdered!"

So it can be understood, after Harrigan's death on

that Saturday in May, that when Grandma Bell prophesied of "much tragic happenings and bloodshed to
come," the long-suffering inhabitants of the Lucan area
could only sigh and prepare for the worst.

It was not long in coming!

On a Wednesday morning following Harrigan's
death — while folks wondered who was next on the
Donnellys' list — the Quigley sisters lumbered their
fat, rheumatic twenty-year-old grey mare, Peg, into
Lucan with yet another brain-reeling story. They too,
like the Ryans, had been visited by four of the dead
Donnellys! In fact, the Donnellys had just left their
house!

The Quigley sisters, two spinsters in their fifties
and both a bit tetched in the head, lived in a small
frame house a short distance from the village, where
they wound up the clock, put out the cat, and, as hope
springs eternal — peeked under the bed nightly for a
prince charming. But no dice. Both were notorious
gossips, but they were not known to be out and out
liars; in other words you could usually believe at least
part of what they said. The story they told was practically the same as the Ryans'. The four Donnellys — old
Jim, Johannah, and sons Tom and John — had walked
into their kitchen shortly after eight that morning —
each carrying a lily and smelling strongly of the grave!

According to the Quigley sisters, the foursome had
remained in the kitchen for the better part of an hour,
sitting on chairs, occasionally talking among themselves but mostly staring at the floor. On leaving,
Johannah had told the spinsters:

"We intended to call on Shiftless Jack Quinn this
Saturday night, but he must have sensed it and had

brains enough to leave the country. From now on, two days before our next raid, at midnight, we will leave a flaming torch burning before the gate of the house of our intended victim. The man who finds it has one of two choices: Either leave the district in forty-eight hours or face the vengeance of the Black Donnellys!"

Then Johannah Donnelly had said: "And now, please pardon us. We are going back to our new home — to rest and plan!"

As the sisters told it, the Donnellys had then walked out of the kitchen, across the yard, climbed over the back fence and started to cut across the fields beyond — and towards the graveyard! Towards their "new home."

It was the same story again. Village tongues worked overtime to spread the tale of the Quigleys; rural folks did the same, and by nightfall the entire countryside had heard of it. Then came the question that caused hours of speculation: who was next; what man was destined to see the torch flaming before his home come Thursday night?

By then the original thirty men were reduced to twenty-seven — two by death, one by flight — and among those remaining was Mike Slattery. Slattery, a widower, was of medium-build, a quarrelsome man with a cancer-eaten nose, who had a perpetual grudge against the world and everyone in it. Bald as a peeled egg and around fifty, hating folks came easy to him; he had been a bitter enemy of the Donnellys for more than a decade and willingly participated in their massacre. More than that, for the past year he had been urging his fellow murderers to "wipe out the three surviving Donnelly brothers — make a complete job of it!"

Mike Slattery had an infrequent caller in his grimy abode, in the equally repulsive person of John Purtell — since even skunks occasionally get together when no one else wants them. Late on a Thursday night, while the countryside wondered before whose home the flaming torch would be tossed, Purtell walked into the Slattery house and greeted its ignoble owner.

"Was ridin' by on my way home from the village, Mike," he said, "and thought I would drop in for a few words. Also a couple of stiff jolts, so trot out the little brown jug." Purtell's eyes went to the kitchen table; saw that the jug had already been trotted out, so he added: "Stay in your seat, Mike and I'll help myself."

"Damn your cheap hide, you always do," grumbled Slattery who was tighter than a snake's arse to the ground. He asked, "What's new in the village; everyone hidin' behind locked doors, afraid of the ghosts of the Donnellys?"

Purtell downed a half-glass of raw spirits in a gulp, refilled the glass and turned to the other with a shrug. "Just about, Mike; there were only six of us in the Western Bar tonight, everyone tight-lipped, nervous as hell and hardly a soul on the streets. Folks seemed to be scared half to death — and all for nothin'."

"Yes, and how do you know it's all for nothin'? What makes you so sure?"

Purtell took a backward step and regarded the other with a puzzled expression before exclaiming: "What the hell? Don't tell me you're startin' to believe all those crazy stories? The devil take you — I thought you were too much of a man for that!"

"If you had a few brains in that empty head of yours, Purtell, you'd give some thought to those stories. I tell you, all hell will soon be poppin' around here. I can feel it in my bones!"

It marked the beginning of an hour of insults and arguments, interrupted by frequent tilting of the jug on the table; midnight was near when John Purtell arose to take his departure. Slattery got to his feet to accompany him to the road; they stepped though the kitchen door into the quiet of a clear May night. A half-moon was directly overhead, the sky agleam with stars, while a wandering wind wafted the fragrance from a nearby lilac bush. But the beauty of the night was lost to that pair of heartless killers, who rarely appreciated anything not connected with violence or cruelty to others. When they reached the gateway, Purtell said to Slattery:

"I'm tellin' you for the last time, Mike, and you can say what you like, but all those stories you've been hearin' are crazy."

"I'm not so sure."

"Well I am, but I'll tell you somethin' else. I've always liked your idea about wipin' out the three remainin' Donnelly brothers and finishin' a much needed job with three good murders. Fact is, I like the idea so much I've decided to speak to the others about it, and see if we can't get 'em to come around to our way of thinkin'!"

Ugly as sin with that cancer-eaten nose, Slattery nodded. "Glad you see it my way; it would be the best thing that could happen for all of us," came his answer. "Yes, and the fastest way to go about it would be..."

His voice halted, then trailed off into silence as a series of sounds reached their ears — galloping hoofs rapidly approaching down the lonely road before them, while a large and dancing flame seemed to be shooting through the darkness and towards that evil pair. Startled exclamations burst from their lips, and the next minute, a long cape fluttering behind her, the Midnight Lady came into view. In her right hand she carried a four-foot pole, one end aflame.

In a wild charge both horse and rider dashed up and came to a sharp stop before the amazed men, as the right hand of the Midnight Lady flew far back over her shoulder. Then that hand shot forward, the pole sped from it in javelin-like fashion — to bury its sharp point directly before the gate and remaining standing with its flaring end aloft. As promised, a torch flamed before a house that night; a four-foot high torch. And then:

"For you, Mike Slattery, may your murderous soul roast in hell — a fiery present from the Black Donnellys!" cried the silvery voice of the Midnight Lady. "You know what it means — it gives you forty-eight hours to get out of this district forever, or face the vengeance of the dead — one so terrible its very mention would pollute the air around us! Heed well, then, the warning of the torch!"

Her gaze rested on Purtell; one gloved hand gestured to him. "A week from tonight I will bring another burning faggot that will be tossed before your house, John Purtell, for you are next on that long list that has been written in blood!"

That was all, the following instant she was off. The great black horse shot ahead into the darkness, while the flurry of hoofs drummed loud, then grew fainter and fainter and finally died away. And the two men before the gate? They listened, tense and speechless, till all was still once more, before they turned to stare at each other in a long two-minute silence. Then, as one, they both wheeled, hurried back into the house

— and made straight towards the little brown jug!

Even today around these parts, there are still a few old-timers who remember the exact location where once stood the Swamp Schoolhouse. Of course there is little or nothing to be seen there now, but eighty years ago it was a different story. Yes, a far different story — then!

You see, for several months before the Donnelly massacre, its perpetrators had held a number of meetings at the Swamp Schoolhouse — and always late at night — where plans were made for the attack. Damnable plans! Murderous plans — conceived by men who were always in a half-drunken state! And it was in that same log-built structure that the killers of the Donnellys met late on the night after the Midnight Lady had tossed the flaming torch into the ground before the home of Mike Slattery. Most of the assembly — workworn and hardened sons of the soil — had received word of the meeting only a few hours earlier, but twenty-four men were assembled there when Dan Larkin mounted the small dais that was the teacher's platform and called for order. In the quiet that followed, Larkin asked:

"There are only twenty-four of us here. Where are Jack Brady, Mike Slattery and John Purtell?"

Someone called out: "Brady told me to tell you he'd be along in a few minutes; he drove over to pick up Purtell and Slattery. But we're here, so suppose you tell us why the hell you had to get us over here at this hour of the night? What is so damned important it can't keep till tomorrow and daylight?"

"Yes — that's right! What's it all about?" came from the assembly.

"I'll damn soon tell you what it's all about and I'll make it brief!" snapped Dan Larkin. "There is a crazy slut ridin' up and down these roads in the darkness, known as the Midnight Lady — and she's got to be stopped! She's got to be stopped even if we have to slit her bastardly throat to do it! That's what it's all about!"

"Who says so?" a voice inquired.

"The Squire," was Larkin's answer, "and as usual he's right. The meddlin' bitch is arousing the entire countryside against the men who killed the Donnellys — which means us! You've heard and I've heard how she pulls up before farmhouses at night, and from the roadway calls out for folks to unite, search out, and drive the murderers of the Donnellys out of the country — or else turn 'em over to the law. She keeps saying it is the duty of folks to bring the killers to justice; they're startin' to believe her. Startin' to think for themselves. Next thing you know, they'll be takin' action and bringin' us before the hangman. So she's got to be stopped if we're to stay alive!"

For the next quarter of an hour Larkin told the others of the orders he had received from Cyrus Robbin. In brief, they had to do with capturing the Midnight Lady — "that meddlin' bitch!" Her presence, he warned, was a menace to all of them; as an added incentive, Cyrus Robbin would pay five hundred dollars in cold cash to the man who could ride her down and deliver her into his hands — "where she will be damn well dealt with as she deserves." So all of them were to keep their eyes open, especially with the coming of night; to have a horse saddled and ready to charge down upon her, the minute she made an appearance. Some of them were bound to see her sooner or later. One of them could make himself five hundred dollars richer — a small fortune to the Canadian farmer of eighty years ago.

"Well, that's it, men," Larkin presently concluded. "You'll not only be savin' your own necks; one or more of you can make a nice piece of money by grabbin' her, tyin' her up and bringin' her to the Squire and me. And when you do — oh, when you do!"

Dan Larkin raised a clenched fist, eyes flashing, swarthy features scowling. "Oh, when that happy day comes and I get my hands on that slut, I can promise you all one thing," he said. "I'll get a poker, heat it till it's blood red — and then I'll brand my initials on her rump!"

The schoolhouse door was flung open and Jack Brady entered, striding forward in the manner of a man bearing important news. Brady, you will recall, was the man who had driven over to the Slattery place to pick up and bring Slattery and Purtell to the meeting. Dan Larkin called out to him: "Oh, it's you, Brady, and about time. Where are the others; where are Slattery and Purtell?"

"They're not comin'."

"Not comin'?"

"That's what I said," was Brady's reply. "They're not comin', now or ever. They've gone — vamoosed — skedaddled!"

Larkin exclaimed: "What the hell are you talking about, you imbecile?"

"Talkin' about what happened, that's what — and plenty did! We all know that the Midnight Lady had warned Slattery and Purtell they were to be the next two victims of Donnelly vengeance. And those fellows sure must have believed her and gone to pieces, both of them, as this letter proves!"

Brady produced a sheet of writing paper, held it up and said:

"No need to read it. It just proves that both of them are gettin' out of the district, and I learned they left for London around sundown. They don't say where they're goin' from there, but it means only one thing. They've gone, and now there are five less than there were before that woman started ridin' up and down the roads after midnight. Let things go on like this much longer and there won't be a damn one of us left around here. We'll either kill ourselves, get killed or high-tail it out of here. And all because that old hellion, Johannah Donnelly — even as we were clubbin' her to death — kept shriekin' we'd all die a violent death! That every one of us would die a violent death, and she'd come back from the grave and haunt us till we did! She kept yellin' it over and over!"

In the shocked silence that followed, someone spoke in a hoarse whisper: "Who knows? Maybe that's just what she is doin' — and has been doin'! Who knows?"

One thing, however, was known: both Slattery and Purtell had fled. Separating in London, Mike Slattery made his way to Windsor where, three weeks later, his throat was slashed from ear to ear with the jagged edges of a broken whisky bottle in a bar-room brawl. John Purtell lasted a bit longer. A seaman in his youth, he journeyed to Toronto, secured a berth as deckhand on a freighter plying the Great Lakes, and five months passed before — with the ship in dock — he tumbled over the railing and was drowned!

It is said that, "He was fished out of the water with a look of horror on his face," And who can tell just what he did see in his final seconds?

CHAPTER TEN

The Coming of the Gypsies

He screamed, 'I see old Johannah now,'
In what was his final breath.
For then he took a backward step,
And toppled to his death.

— Old Song —

May blushed itself out, June blushed itself in, then the gypsies came to the long-suffering Lucan district. It heralded, "a tragedy that was to make the countryside bow its head in shame and shock decency to the core!"

However, late one night a week before their arrival, the Midnight Lady had ridden up, dismounted and entered the home of William Donnelly, where William, along with his wife and brothers Pat and Robert, were awaiting her expected visit. As formerly agreed, the blinds were drawn, her horse hidden in the shed, and the family watchdog posted on the porch to warn of any intruders. Such trysts had been a weekly habit for the past several months, and in the small Donnelly parlor the Midnight Lady told them:

"Everything is going exactly as I planned; even now fear is tugging at the hearts of all the Donnelly killers, with each wondering who will be next to face Donnelly vengeance. And the strain, the uncertainty of it all, is telling on them. Already, two have destroyed themselves — one by suicide, one by accident — while three more, terrorized, have fled the district, but doomed to be haunted by their conscience — till the end of their days!"

She leaned forward, masked and glorious, her red lips parted like a rose's petals about to fall apart, as she added: "Best of all, not one of you brothers have had to as much as lift a hand or strike a single blow in retaliation — and yet your enemies are fleeing before you, while the few who do remain are panic-stricken!"

William Donnelly gave a ruefull smile, shrugged his shoulders and admitted: "Sure, an' all I've had to do was drive my old nag to Lucan and back a few times, play the fiddle and let Paddy squawk, dance and flap his wings on my shoulder."

"Well it's not like the old days, I will admit that," put in Robert Donnelly. "Then it was different; then we had to fight fire with fire, clubs with clubs, fists with fists, all hell with all hell."

"Let's hope those days are no more," interrupted the Midnight Lady. "Have I not proved to you that violence is unnecessary — that common sense and playing on the superstition of others are far more powerful weapons than brawn and brute force? Don't you see that?"

"The truth, indeed it is," put in Nora, "and we can never thank you enough for what you have done for us, young lady, but don't you really think — well — er — isn't it about time that you finally told us why — why —"

The Midnight Lady gave her musical laugh. "Once again you want to ask me why I am doing what I do," came her reply. "And once more I have to answer that the time has not yet come when I can reveal the reason for it all. Someday, soon now, perhaps; but in the meanwhile —"

She began to outline her plans for the nights ahead — uncertain nights, dangerous nights — while around her the four Donnellys, all attention, listened to the words of the tall, shapely beauty. From his nearby perch, Paddy the crow looked on in silence.

The caravan of the gypsies consisted of three heavy wagons, two cows, fourteen horses and eleven humans. Among the latter was Anita. Tall, dark-eyed and beautiful Anita!

Beside a small stream in a wooded glen, some three miles from the village and not a great way from the present hamlet of Clandeboye, the caravan came to a halt on that June day in 1881; several small tents were staked out and raised, while large black cooking pots appeared and yells came from iron-lunged kids with dirty faces. Of course such a company was a fairly common sight in the Canada of eighty years ago, and this one was no exception from the general rule. They had come there for the men folks to trade and sell horses, while the women told fortunes and all of them took turns in stealing vegetables from surrounding fields and raiding nearby chicken coops.

Beautiful Anita, aged nineteen and with the grace of a fallen leaf, was the daughter of Kibo, the stocky and swarthy kingpin of the outfit, whose toothless wife had a face that would curdle a mare's milk. Anita's younger brothers and sisters — there were seven of them — ranged in age from five to seventeen, with the remaining member of the group being her uncle, a shifty-eyed character whose trained fingers had lifted many a wallet and watch — sometimes both — from the pockets of unsuspecting Canadians for close on to two decades. But as mentioned, the group was no exception to the average band of gypsies roving the broad expanse of Canada eighty years ago. To be brief, they weren't exactly honest but they wouldn't steal anything that was nailed down or invisible.

Right from the start — that is to say, two days after their arrival in the district — dark-eyed Anita had made a crashing impression upon the young bloods of the village when she made her first visit to Lucan for supplies. The rural lads had never seen anything that could even begin to approach this hot-blooded, hip-swaying gypsy beauty, who, dressed in the finery of her tribe, was arrayed in more colors than you could find in a dozen rainbows — not to mention some five pounds of cheap jewelry. But to these young Casanovas, she was Cleopatra returned to life, just stepped off her barge.

Believe me, brother, a lot of schemes were hatched in the brains of the young fellows who beheld her — and not all of them were exactly nice. Come to think of it, probably none of them were. And, as though to encourage said schemes, Anita made it very apparent with her ready smile and bedroom eyes — not to mention those swaying hips — that she was a girl who liked attention.

That same night several Romeos were so bold as to ride out to the caravan and approach the gypsy campfire. When their purpose became known, old Kibo appeared with his shotgun, which was enough to cool passion and sent the daring young men riding away into the darkness. Romance took a bad beating that

night, but as the dejected youths made their way
homeward they were comforted by the fact that there
was always tomorrow.

A week or so passed, then came the Saturday afternoon when Dan Larkin drove Cyrus Robbin into
Lucan. Massive Mr. Robbin had several business calls
to make on local merchants, while Larkin spent the
two hours drinking heavily as was his custom. Jack
Brady, one of the men who helped massacre the
Donnellys, walked up to him, features serious, and
spoke in a quiet voice. They were in the Western Bar.

"Dan, you know that the flaming torch was burning
before Shawn Murphy's home last Thursday night?"

Larkin nodded and said:

"Yes, but there's nothin' to worry about. Murphy's
got guts; he won't panic. Besides, I and a dozen of the
boys will be out to his house before midnight, come
Saturday, just to see that all goes well with him. Us
fellows have got to stick together. Say, Jack," went on
Larkin, "suppose you bring your gun and be there?
There'll be lots to drink after midnight; we plan to
throw a party — all of us will get drunk as old hell —
after we've proven there's no truth about dead
Donnellys gettin' vengeance."

"Yes?" asked Jack Brady.

With that, Jack Brady downed his drink, called for
a refill and, as Larkin watched, sent it down the hatch.
Then Brady took a deep breath. First he looked at the
ceiling, then at the bar mirror, after which his gaze
traveled down to his shoes, and up to the eyes of the
other. Brady spoke in almost a whisper:

"No, I won't be at Murphy's Saturday night, Larkin,
and there isn't any reason why you or the others should
be there either. You see, I just came from the Murphy

place less than thirty minutes ago and helped his wife carry him from the barn into the house. Talk about blood — you've never seen anything like it! His face was so gory you'd have thought someone splashed it with red paint! You're the first I've told; didn't want to panic the others."

"Shawn Murphy!" exclaimed Larkin. "What are you saying; you mean he's — he's —."

"Dead as a mackerel!" ejaculated Brady. "Accordin' to his wife, he'd gone out to the stable to curry that balky roan of his. He was three sheets to the wind; the damn fool put his lighted pipe on the horse's rump, forgot it was there, and the nag lashed out with a powerful kick and the hoof and horseshoe crashed full into Murphy's face!"

As Larkin stared at him in wide-eyed surprise, Brady added: "Now there are only twenty-four of us left, Dan. Yes — and I'm gettin' frightened! I've a feelin' I'm next!"

When Dan Larkin, his face flushed and a bit wobbly on his pins, left the bar and returned to the Robbin buggy to await his employer, it was to find a magnificent coal-black saddle horse tethered beside it on the long hitching rail in front of one of the stores. Larkin was admiring the animal, as he had on the former occasion he had seen it, when Cyrus Robbin approached him.

Larkin gestured to the beast. "Real horse-flesh there," he said. "Wouldn't mind having that critter myself, and I'll lay odds that in a race he'll show his black rear to any nag in this district."

Cyrus Robbin let his gaze wander towards the horse in a bored manner — and suddenly he didn't seem bored. Instead a look of interest came to his face. He inspected the legs, and teeth; he ran one hand down the animal's glossy back before he turned to Larkin and said:

"I'll wager this fellow has the speed of the wind." Then he asked: "Do you know who owns him?"

Dan Larkin chuckled. "I sure do and she's even more interestin' to look at than her horse. I hear her name's Anita; she's one of those gypsies camped in the glen about three miles north of here; I first laid eyes on her when I was in the village last Wednesday, and let me tell you she's somethin' to look at."

Larkin gave a short laugh, shot one of his characteristic quick glances over his shoulder and went on: "You ought to see her, she's got everythin' and then some. Wavy black hair; eyes dark and smilin'. Her behind sways like a lazy fan — your hands itch to pat it — and her bubbies bounce and roll with every step she takes. I'm tellin' you, she can jump in bed with me anytime she wants to."

Cyrus Robbin gave a knowing nod. "So can just about any other woman in the world. You're not fussy that way, are you?"

Larkin gave a frank reply, "Never was, never intend to be; I take what comes my way and ask no questions." He checked a thumb in the direction of the store and said, "Here comes that gypsy wench now!"

All sex and curves, dressed in her garments of many colors, the girl swung into her saddle with an ease that spoke of long practice, while a dozen open-mouthed yokels looked on. Cyrus Robbin stepped forward to doff his black hat and politely say: "This horse of yours, young lady; he's quite an animal."

Anita the gypsy nodded, smiled but said nothing.

However, the smile and her silence must have encouraged the other, for he came closer to ask: "Perhaps you might be interested in selling him? Is he for sale?"

The shake of her head did not discourage him, for Cyrus Robbin was a persistent cuss as well as an experienced horse trader. He manufactured a smile and said: "Oh, come now, you should reflect on the matter before you reply, and besides, everything has its price." He declared, "I'll pay you good money for this horse, probably more money than you have ever seen before at any one time in your life. Well, what do you say? Name your own price."

"He's not for sale." The answer came in a soft, youthful voice. "No; there is not enough money in the world to take Black Brook away from me."

Cyrus Robbin rubbed his soft white hands together and purred, "No? And why not?"

She shrugged. "Because I need him. Maybe, because I know when I have him beneath me, that no one is ever going to catch me unless I want them to. Yes — that's the reason I won't sell him. No one can ever catch me or hope to when I'm riding Black Brook, and both he and I know it. Yes, and I think you know it, too, sir."

A knowing smile appeared on the face of Cyrus Robbin. Eyes narrowed, he spoke in that soft voice of his. "Yes, I realized as much and I expected you to speak exactly as you did. Your words have told me a great deal; much more than you think they have."

Standing nearby, swarthy Dan Larkin heard the reply of Cyrus Robbin and stared at him in surprise. Then Larkin wheeled to the gypsy girl.

"What the hell's the matter with you, you brainless wench?" demanded Larkin. "Mr. Robbin wants the horse so sell it to him, make yourself some money and stop the gabbin'. Then after the sale I'll drive you back to the camp; yes, and maybe on the way we can stop and rest for a while in the thick clusters of maples, a mile out of town. What do you say?"

He stepped forward, raised a hand, gave her thigh a playful pat and inquired, "Like the idea — you tantalizin' minx?"

She didn't, and proved as much in a manner that was to be discussed for years by those who saw what followed. And it happened with a speed almost too fast for the eye to follow. As Larkin came out with his vile proposition, the right hand of the gypsy maid flew to her garments, whipped out a sparkling dagger the sharp point of which was suddenly an inch from Larkin's throat.

"Pig! Donnelly killer!" cried Anita. "Another word from your evil throat and I slit it as though it were paper!"

No matter what else he was, Dan Larkin was no coward; he had proven that many times. But as that wicked-looking blade shot towards him, his eyes snapped wide and he hurriedly took a backward step. Then, at a shrill whistle from its owner, the horse, Black Brook, wheeled, snorted, rose on its hind legs and two front hoofs flayed the air scant inches from Larkin's face. He lept back farther as the girl tugged at the bridle reigns of her charger.

"The next time I won't hold him back, Donnelly killer," shouted Anita. "The next time I will let him trample your skull to powder and your flesh to shreds!"

She turned her mount and rode off in an outburst of speed that left onlookers staring in mute surprise. As for Dan Larkin, he shouted out a vile oath after the departing rider, then bounded to the nearby buggy and leaped into it, as though intending to give chase. He might have, too, if Cyrus Robbin had not called out a sharp order. Then Robbin joined him in the buggy and the pair drove out of the village in silence.

A mile down the road the Squire broke the silence with: "An interesting scene back there in the village, Larkin, and most informative. It told me a great deal."

Larkin gave a surly, "Yeah? Well, that gypsy bitch sure told plenty about me. Shouted out to the whole damn village that I was a Donnelly killer. 'You're a Donnelly killer,' she yelled, and come to think of it, she said it twice — the slut! Now just how the hell did she know?"

The other waved a hand to silence him. Cyrus Robbin went on: "It makes no difference how she knows; practically the whole village knows and some- one must have told her. But that is of no immediate importance, nor is the fact that you made an ass of yourself before the villagers."

Larkin sought to change the subject. "By the way, sir, did you hear about Shawn Murphy?"

"I know all about it; unfortunate but not impor- tant," broke in Cyrus Robbin. He cleared his throat and said: "Larkin, listen to me! I believe an almost unbelievable bit of good luck has fallen into our hands."

Larkin became interested. "It has?"

"Indeed it has — without doubt," went on the other, a certain triumph in his voice, a twinkle in his eyes. "In fact, Larkin, I believe a streak of luck — and one from the blue — has enabled us to solve all our problems! My keen sense of observation and sound judgement did the rest. Brought about the downfall of our greatest enemy!"

"And what does that mean?" asked Larkin.

"Just that I was able to learn the true identity of the gypsy girl. Would you like to know who she really is?"

"I would."

"Then get ready for a big surprise, Larkin. She is none other than the Midnight Lady!"

"What?" exclaimed Dan Larkin. He pulled the horses to a sharp halt, turned and stared at the other. "Come again; what's that you're saying?"

Cyrus Robbin nodded. "Oh yes; there is no doubt about it," was his confident answer. He leaned forward.

"You remember, I once had an encounter with the Midnight Lady. On that occasion she was masked, of course, but she did speak; I remember her voice, so that's why I pretended to be interested in the gypsy girls' horse, so I could hear her voice again when I bartered for it." He gave a chuckle. "And she fell for my little scheme, Larkin, betrayed herself, and now I know that the gypsy girl is in reality the Midnight Lady. As to her horse, I recognized it at once."

Larkin exclaimed, "I'll be damned," then: "Well since we know who she is, what do we do now? Call some of the boys together, ride out to the gypsy camp at once and grab her?"

Cyrus Robbin raised a hand though he continued to smile. "Not so fast, my good fellow. There is no need to rush our victory for several reasons I will explain later. No, we will let things go on as they are for a few more days," he confided. "There are a few little matters I wish to check up on before we take her. But when we do — well, what I'll do to her then will be delightful!"

Cyrus Robbin nodded to the horses. "Now whip up the team, Larkin, and hurry me home. I intend to have several stiff drinks of my best brandy, eat a hearty meal and then have my first good night's sleep in three months!"

Old Doc MacCarthy never did forget that long-gone Saturday, and years later he would frequently recall it.

"That was a day I'll remember if I live to be a hundred. Early in the afternoon I was asked to drive out to the farm of Shawn Murphy, where I found Murphy dead from a kick in the head by a horse. I returned to Lucan just in time to see the gypsy girl, Anita, pull out a dagger and threaten to plunge it into the throat of Dan Larkin. A short while later I men Jack Brady, more than a bit tipsy, as he made his way from the saloon, and Brady — known to be a Donnelly killer — confided to me that he had a feeling he was not long for this world. That he was to be the next victim of Donnelly vengeance!"

"And believe it or not," old Doc would declare, "just before sundown a boy galloped up to my place, said I was wanted at the Brady place, and I went out and found Jack Brady dead. His old mother who lived with him, told me that Brady had gone up to the barn roof to replace several shingles. That all at once he started to scream, act crazy and shout that the ghost of old Johannah Donnelly was coming to get him. He said he could see her and she was covered with blood! He fell off the barn roof and broke his back!"

The death of Jack Brady reduced the number of living Donnelly killers in the Lucan district to twenty-three.

CHAPTER ELEVEN

While the Campfire Burned Low

They crept up to the gypsy camp
In the glen, when all was still.
Then while stars gleamed, as one the twelve,
Rushed in wildly for the kill.

— Old Song —

Early on the Tuesday morning, following the momen-
tous Saturday so often recalled by old Doc McCarthy in
later years, still another event shocked the inhabitants
of Lucan. Sometime during the previous night, a party
or parties unknown, had painted no less than twenty-
three front doors of various houses throughout the
district with blood-red, three-foot high letters:

D.K.

Needless to say, everyone for miles around knew
that D.K. could signify only one thing: Donnelly Killer!
And as later facts proved, each home so adorned, was
either owned by or housed a man who had been a
member of the mob on that terrible night. There had
been no mistakes.

Of course the identity of every Donnelly killer had
not been known — only guessed at — by most of the
folks of the district, and once the word got around as

to what had happened, what followed could best be described as a holiday for sightseers. The news spread. Farmers left fields that needed their attention, housewives deserted their kitchens and merchants their stores, as they took to driving around the countryside to find out which houses had the sign. The identity of some of the owners shocked folks to the core.

Not only that, five of the homes were in Lucan itself, with one owner being none other than a highly respected and recently elected village official!

The door of Dan Larkin's small house, a mile from that of his employer, was smeared with a large D.K.!

But nothing had been painted on the door of Cyrus Robbin's home; it had been left untouched and in a way it was only proper, since that wily gent had made it a point to be sure that he was miles away from the massacre at the time of its occurrence. So far none but his hirelings — the actual killers themselves — knew of his connection with the murders or the fact that it was none other than his three-hundred-pound self which had been the mastermind behind it all. He was still regarded as the community's leading citizen and no one, absolutely no one — not even his trusted henchman, Dan Larkin — knew, suspected, guessed or had even the faintest idea why he had ordered the slaughter of the Donnellys. Yes — and he chuckled at the thought — that was his secret, his secret alone.

And in all truth, nobody did know the reason. That is, nobody knew but the Midnight Lady!

Around noon on that Tuesday, Dan Larkin galloped up to the home of Cyrus Robbin, dust-covered, his horse lathered. He hurried into the study where the Squire awaited him with raised bushy eyebrows.

"Well?"

"The jig's up for the boys and me — we're gone goslin's now!" exclaimed Larkin, breathing hard. "I went to the homes of all of them; been ridin' hell-for-leather for the past four hours, and that bitch of a Midnight Lady — along with whoever it was that helped her — painted those damned D.K. letters on the doors of the houses of all of us!"

"Go on."

"Go on? Hell, what more is there to say?" asked Larkin, wide-eyed and worried. "Now everyone knows who the killers are; all there is for them and me to do is just sit on our rears and wait till a bunch of John Laws come in from London, and cart the lot of us off to meet the noose. I'll lay odds that all of us will have to tread air at the end of a rope before the leaves fall!"

Cyrus Robbin inquired: "Those D.K. letters? Are you sure it was the work of the Midnight Lady?"

"Of course! It couldn't have been anyone else! It's just another of her tricks!"

Then Larkin exploded: "Damn it all to hell, it's goin' to come true, just like that blatherskite of a grand-mother of mine used to say! She always said I'd end my days on the gallows! That's the part that hurts me the most, and I'll bet the slut grins when I meet her in hell!"

Larkin turned to the other, accusing: "You know, I blame you for this. Last Saturday, when we were drivin' back from the village and you told me you had learned that the gypsy girl was the Midnight Lady, I wanted to get some of the boys, ride out to the camp then and there and grab her. If I had, she wouldn't have been able to do all this paintin' business. But you said no; you said you wanted to wait awhile before we took her. Remember?"

Cyrus Robbin nodded and spoke calmly: "A regrettable error on my part, but it does not necessarily mean the end of the world. Now Larkin, sit down; relax and you'll last longer. I've something to tell you that can still pull our chestnuts out of the fire."

"It had better be good," put in the other.

According to Cyrus Robbin, it was good, very good — his plan to save the remaining twenty-three Donnelly killers. In fact it was so good, he said, that no one else could have thought of it. He went on to say that immediate and drastic steps would have to be taken; but if this were done — and done exactly as he said it should be done — there was still hope for the murderers. A case of there's corn in Egypt yet. And he must have been a convincing talker. When he finished, at the end of thirty minutes, a look of confidence spread across Dan Larkin's face.

When Larkin finally rose to leave, promising to carry out all orders to the letter, Cyrus Robbin rose too and accompanied him to the gate.

And, once again, just outside the window, little Danny Doyle got to his feet, a far-away look in his eyes. He had overheard all that had been said and knew that early that evening, his day's work over, he would have an important message to deliver. A most important message!

Around eleven that night, with a full moon sailing across the sky, Dan Larkin and eleven other men — D.Ks, all of them — pulled their horses off the road a hundred yards from the glen where the gypsies were encamped. Through the trees ahead they could see the glow of a campfire.

At a word from Larkin, they dismounted and gathered around him — hardened and desperate men, each of whom felt he was just one jump ahead of the scaffold. And desperate men become dangerous men who will do just about anything.

Larkin spoke, quietly but rapidly: "Now I'm going' over it again, so there can be no slip-up. The Squire says our one hope is to get this gypsy wench, for she is the Midnight Lady — the one who, right now, has us all up that well-known creek."

"Yes, we know, we're to seize her, tie her up and take her to Cyrus Robbin," broke in one of the men. "That's it, isn't it?"

"Right, Connors," came Larkin's reply. "We'll take her to the Squire — after I get through with her. As to the rest of the gypsies, we'll rough 'em up plenty, frighten hell out of and send them runnin' from this district — forever. When we get through with them, they'll think twice before comin' back."

"Go on," spoke Connors.

Larkin did so: "Well, then we'll just sit tight, all of us, deny we had anything to do with the Donnelly murders and hope for the best. The Squire told me to tell you that. Once we get that meddlin' Midnight Lady out of the way, maybe we'll have some peace around here and the massacre will be forgotten. Sure hope it is. I'm tired of stayin' awake nights, worryin' about the hangman!"

"What's the Squire going to do with the girl, after he gets her?" asked Connors.

"Who the hell cares what he does with her as long as he gets rid of her?" snapped Dan Larkin. "Think of savin' your own hides, Connors, not about what will happen to hers." Then he ordered: "All right men, put those handkerchiefs I gave you around your faces and we'll get this one over with quick. We don't want those gypsies to be able to recognize any of us if we should ever run into them again."

The air around that unholy lot reeked with fumes of alcohol. A few were unsteady on their feet; the noticeable bulge on the hip of each told that every man had ample supply of liquor with him. This of course was deemed most proper on such occasions. For weapons, all of them carried a stout club, the accepted implement of the district and the weapons of their ancestors. Someone suggested it was time they had a drink, and there was not a single protest. Bottles were produced, corks drawn, heads tilted back and gurgling sounds ensued.

Then, large, bright-colored handkerchiefs were tied around the face of each, after which Larkin spoke again:

"Connors, Flynn and Brannigan, you swing around the woods, walk quietly and come in on the camp from the rear, just in case some of the bastards make a run for it. We mustn't give them any chance to get away till we deal with them. I'll allow the three of you five minutes to get in place, then the rest of us will charge in on them, yellin' like hell, clubs swingin'!"

The camp of the gypsies was in a small clearing, surrounded by heavy brush and trees. As mentioned, there were eleven of them. There was Kibo, the leader, his ugly wife and his brother, as well as Kibo's beautiful daughter Anita, and her seven younger sisters and brothers.

As the oncoming raiders drew closer, five figures could be seen around the dying embers of the camp-fire, behind which were the three heavy wagons that sheltered the six younger and sleeping members of the group. Kibo, reclining and with head supported by one hand, smoked his pipe as he mentally reviewed the success of his horse trading in the past ten days; beside him his brother did the same. Kibo's wife, after a hard day of supervising six squalling and squabbling youngsters, sat beneath a tree, allowing herself the brief luxury of forty winks. Nearby, beautiful nineteen-year-old Anita sat on a rotting log with Tony her brother, two years her junior.

A strikingly handsome lad with wavy black hair, inch-long eyelashes and delicate features, Tony's long, tapering fingers proclaimed him to be the musician that he was. Gazing up into the starlit night, he was telling his sister:

"It is a night made for dreaming, Anita, while the rest of the world sleeps, unmindful of its beauty. Such ingratitude."

The girl gave a soft laugh. "You are the dreamer, Tony; you always have been. You pay so little attention to the present and what is happening all around you, as though you were living in another world. Perhaps that's why I love you so much."

He went on, eyes still upward. "Have you ever stopped to think, dear sister, what can be beyond those stars we see, so many, many million miles away? Now there has to be something beyond them; perhaps other stars just as distant to them as they are to us." His gaze went to her.

"But if so, what is beyond those distant stars?" he questioned and shook his head. "There has to be an end to it all somewhere," he pointed out. "There has to be an end to everything, even to the giant vastness overhead that we call space."

He stopped and turned to her, his delicate features serious. "All right, and if there finally is an end to space, then what can be beyond that ending — and what holds it all up?"

She ran her fingers through his hair, amusement in her eyes, as she answered: "Why do you always ponder such fantastic problems? The stars are away up there, we are down here and nothing can change it. They are lovely to look at, they are distant worlds; but our own life span down here is too brief, too precious, Tony, to dream away hours of it on the problems of space. Mysteries we can never hope to solve, and perhaps were never meant to."

"But, Anita —"

"Think only of your music, Tony. You have been given a rare gift; you must take full advantage of it. One day you will be playing your violin in huge halls throughout the world, while the high and mighty applaud you, and I will be so proud of you. That is what you should be thinking of, my brother, not the stars or the mysteries of the void overhead. Just your music, always your music and —"

Suddenly from somewhere out in the darkness came the sharp, crackling sound of a snapping branch. It was followed by four loud hoots of an owl. Then silence again. A stillness that was too still. An ominous silence.

Those sounds had had a strange effect on the five gypsies around the campfire, those five wandering children of the highways and byways. As one they got to their feet, gathered together around the glowing embers while sending sharp glances stabbing into the darkness around them. It was quite apparent that they sensed danger. Shena, wife of Kibo, put a finger to her lips, slumping to a crouching position, ears strained for some tell-tale noise. She shook her head when she heard none, before she turned to the others, speaking in a half-whisper:

"I don't like it. No forest creature would be so stupid as to step on and break a branch, and if it is humans that are out there, you can be sure they are up to no good, coming here at such an hour and trying to steal upon us." Her eyes went to Kibo:

"Get your gun and hurry," she said, "for those four hoots of the owl were a warning; I have a terrible feeling that great danger of some kind is around us and approaching. Haste, then, my husband, if we are to —"

She got no further. For at the same instant, from out of the darkness ahead, came the loud, hoarse shouting of: "All right, boys, charge in and get 'em — every damn one of 'em!" The next moment, handkerchiefs concealing their faces, twelve howling men, each carrying a club, ran from the blackness of the surrounding trees and charged the encampment!

CHAPTER TWELVE

"You Can't Reason with Rattlesnakes"

It happened back in eighty-one,
And years have passed since then.
But Lucan's elders still tell of,
That horror in the glen.

— Old Song —

"Line 'em up; line up those thievin' gypsy bastards, every damn last one of 'em — and kick their tails up to their shoulders if they don't hurry! Make 'em look hump-backed!"

It was the harsh voice of brutal Dan Larkin bawling out these words that night in the glen, less than two minutes after he and his shouting, half-drunken followers had rushed in on the gypsy encampment on that June night in 1881.

The surprise attack had been a complete success; little or no resistance had been offered other than a futile attempt on the part of Kibo. But a treacherous and backhand wack from Larkin's club had plunged him, bleeding and half conscious, to the ground. Pulled to his feet, Kibo, his wife, brother, Anita and Tony, were lined up before the campfire. Two of the raiders then brought the remaining members of the family from the wagons where they had been slumbering. They were six very frightened youngsters.

Kibo, the leader, had a number of faults but cowardice was not one of them. Blood flowing down one cheek from the ugly gash across his temple caused by Larkin's club, Kibo could see the members of his family held in the strong hands of the masked raiders and realized that he could expect no mercy. But he drew himself erect and turned to Dan Larkin, who had been shouting out orders to his followers.

"What means this?" he demanded. "You and these men rush in on us, howling like wild devils — and for what? I demand an answer! We have done nothing!"

Larkin gave a harsh laugh. "No; you and the likes of you haven't been doin' a thing, have you?" he shouted. "Just been driftin' around the country for years, cheatin' and thievin' from honest, law-abidin' men, like me and these gentlemen with me."

Dan Larkin shook his clenched fist in the gypsy's face. "Well, when we get through with you, you're goin' to think twice before comin' to this district again."

Then Larkin wheeled to Anita, who was held in the strong grasp of one of the raiders.

"As for you, you slut!" he roared, "you're goin' to wish you were never born. You see, we know you're the Midnight Lady; yes, and there will be no more meddlin' in things that don't concern you, or any more of your night rides — after I get through with you! In fact, I doubt if you will be able to sit your rear in a saddle for months to come, once I've dealt with you — for that's the kind of a hairpin I be!

"By the way," he added, "when it's over I'm takin' you with us!"

The dark eyes of Anita the gypsy girl widened as she

stared at him. Then realization seemed to come to her for she cried: "Why, you're crazy! That's what you are — stark raving crazy!" She wheeled to the other raiders, calling out: "Yes, and the rest of you must be crazy, or you would not follow the orders of this madman! Haven't you got minds of your own?"

Larkin chuckled: "Yes, I'm crazy — crazy like a fox!" Then he snapped: "Now shut up, you young heifer, till I've dealt with the others!" He warned: "And none of your lip or you'll get the back of my hand — so you will!"

Some grim minutes followed, while twigs and wood were tossed on the campfire till it flared up again and orange-colored flames crackled as they leaped skyward.

At Larkin's order, two of the raiders forced Kibo to a slender tree and tied his arms around it, after which his shirt was torn from his back. Then Dan Larkin stepped forward, with the whip he had fashioned for the purpose that very afternoon — a short-handled, devilish-looking thing, with a hole-punctured, two-foot square of hard and heavy leather, that could slash a man's flesh to hamburger. And it did just that while the gypsy youngsters screamed in terror, and Kibo's wife, held by one of the raiders, made the glen ring with her wild wails. Twenty times in all that cruel flogging device crashed across the lacerated back of the gypsy, while crimson drops and bits of flesh shot upward and sideways.

As Larkin concluded his hellish work, Kibo, who had undergone the agony with set jaws and the bravery of a Spartan, slumped forward, unconscious. Then he was cut down, his brother brought forward and a similar sentence carried out. Once more the lash rose and fell!

With the two gypsy men bleeding and helpless, Dan Larkin took it on himself to search the wagons but found little or nothing of value, though the discovery of a violin seemed to interest him. He carried it in one hand — club in the other — when he returned to the campfire and to the captives being held there. Larkin demanded of Anita:

"Well, whose is it? Who the hell owns the fiddle?"

There was no fear in the girl's eyes nor a tremor in her voice as she said: "It belongs to my brother, Tony. It has been in our family for generations. It's nearly two hundred years old and it is his life."

For the first time Dan Larkin paused to take a long look at Tony, the gypsy youth with the sensitive features, wavy black hair and tapering fingers. Then Larkin gave a snort of contempt. "So you're Tony, eh?" he jeered. "Hell, you look more like a girl than a boy to me." He laughed. "Yes, Tony; you're real cute, you are, and you know somethin'? I wouldn't be at all surprised if you perfume yourself, wear petticoats and —"

"Larkin!" broke in one of the raiders, "let's do what we have to do and get out of here. Don't drag the damn thing out!"

Larkin wheeled to the speaker. "Shut up. Tim Flynn," he ordered. "This is my show; I'm runnin' it my way. Start buttin' in and you'll get a smashed face!"

Tony's mother raised tear-filled eyes to implore Larkin: "Do not take my son's violin. Someday he will be a great artist and he will need it. He has never known another."

For the first time, Tony spoke up in a halting, nervous manner: "My — my violin, sir — please be careful with it." The young gypsy half extended his arms. "May I have it — my only possession? Give it to me, please."

"Sure, Tony, I'll give it to you. Sure," was Larkin's reply. "Here it is — you damn half-and-half!"

With that, Larkin brought the violin down upon the head of the gypsy youth with a force that smashed it to pieces. Tony gave a sob of horror, his mother screamed and fell to her knees, reaching for the broken pieces of the fiddle. As for Anita, she stared hard at Larkin, clenched both fists then exclaimed:

"You scum! For nearly two centuries the music of that violin brought joy to thousands throughout Europe and elsewhere; it is said to have been played once in the court of a king and now you have destroyed it — you barbarian! You're lower than an animal!"

Larkin chuckled, pleased with himself as well as her outburst of temper. "Ah, that's what I like, girlie, lots of fightin' spirit in my women. It makes their kisses sweeter when you finally get 'em and —"

One of the raiders called out: "Don't forget that horse you were telling us about."

Dan Larkin had no intention of doing that. He temporarily lost interest in the gypsy girl and walked over to the far end of the clearing, where eight or so horses were tethered to the long rope which in turn was tied to two trees. But Larkin had only one horse in mind and quickly found it — Black Brook, Anita's fleet-footed and prized charger. Nearby was the girl's bridle, blanket and saddle, which Larkin drew on the animal; then he led it back to the campfire, to proclaim to the raiders:

"Well, this is the horse I was tellin' you about, boys — the fastest damn thing on four legs in these parts. Yes, and since these gypsies probably stole him — and we'll never be able to trace the rightful owner — I'm hereby claimin' him as mine from now on. And that's that!"

Then he challenged his followers with: "Any of you men with objections, spit 'em out and I'll deal with 'em now!"

There were no objections.

At this point, you might be wondering about the exact looks of Dan Larkin. Oh, I've said he was tall, husky and swarthy — yes, and not a bad looking fellow in a mannish sort of way — but so are thousands of other men, and I can best describe Larkin by way of comparison with someone whose likeness you have probably seen a hundred times. Now I'm not much of a man for shows; fact is, I have never seen a movie or stage play in my life, but about seven years ago, in Lucan, I came across a discarded movie magazine, and was idly thumbing through the pages when my heart leaped to my mouth. For there, looking right at me, was the picture of one I could have sworn was the Dan Larkin I knew way back in 1881. But it wasn't; it was a picture of a well-known movie actor.

However, I can tell you that Dan Larkin and this actor could have passed for twins. They looked that much alike. Alike as peas in a pod!

When none of his followers objected to his ownership of the horse, Dan Larkin gave Black Brook's rump a pat of approval, mumbled something about how he had just acquired "great horse flesh," then turned to the gypsy girl and said:

"Now I'm going to deal with you, girlie — and in a way you'll never forget!"

Next, he spoke hurriedly to his followers, after first suggesting they all "have a stiff bang for luck." They agreed; bottles were produced, corks drawn and rye juice guzzled. Then Dan Larkin said that in capturing

Anita, they had done a great night's work, "for she is the one known as the Midnight Lady, the slut who took it on herself to seek revenge for the Donnellys, and did her damnedest to put a noose around our necks!" He also reminded them that it was the Midnight Lady who had had those D.K. letters painted upon their homes and brought shame to them all. She had let the whole district know that they were Donnelly killers. When Tim Flynn suggested they get going and take her to Cyrus Robbin, Dan Larkin wheeled to the speaker:

"Not so fast, Flynn," he ordered. "Sure we'll take her to the Squire, but first, don't you remember what I promised you fellows a while back at the Swamp Schoolhouse? I said — and I meant every word of it — that if I ever laid hands on the Midnight Lady I'd brand my initials on her rump and —

"Well," he demanded, "I've got her now, haven't I?"

But that was too much even for the hardened and heartless gang of killers who had followed Larkin into the glen that night. Fierce objections rose from the lips of all of them, and as one of the masked men put it, "For us to permit you to do such a thing would stamp us even lower than we are now."

But Larkin stood firm. He said that when he promised to do anything he always made it a point to do it. He added that this time was going to be no exception, even though the heavens fell. He even went so far as to look around, find, pick up and toss a discarded horseshoe into the now blazing campfire; apparently with every intention of using it as a branding iron. However, it was just as evident his followers intended that such should not be the case. Their shouted protests rose higher, louder — and angrier!

Tim Flynn yelled out: "Larkin, I'll see you in hell before I'll permit you to put a red-hot horseshoe on that girl's behind!"

Larkin howled. "Damn the lot of you, for a bunch of spineless whelps! No guts in any of you — just spineless whelps! And as for you, Flynn, maybe you've forgotten the hidin' I gave you last year? And the one two years before that? If I have to give you another, it will be a real son of a bitch!"

"I haven't forgotten, Dan, but this time the others are with me," was Flynn's answer. "So unless you think you can take on eleven of us, you will leave that girl alone."

"And I might do just that, damn you, if I have to!" came the sharp reply.

Anita's mother, aware of the hideous danger that threatened her daughter, was again making the glen ring with her loud wails and frantic prayers to the gods of her ancestors. The gypsy youngsters were crying while Tony wrung his hands. Kibo, returned to consciousness, had struggled back to his family and was hoarsely pleading for his daughter; his lacerated back a fearsome sight in the glow of the leaping flames. But the dark-eyed Anita showed no fear nor begged for mercy. Instead, she showed her scorn and hatred for the raiders, finally turning to her father with:

"Do not plead with them!" she cried. "You cannot plead with or reason with rattlesnakes! Rattlesnakes know only to kill, want only to kill; yes, and they go right on doing it till they themselves are killed. You can expect nothing else so don't waste your breath! You can't reason with rattlesnakes!"

Her words stung Dan Larkin. He gave a half-leap in the air, and a vile oath shot from his lips before he shrieked, "Rattlesnakes?! Then he stepped towards Anita, raised a clenched fist and yelled:

"Another word out of you, you cheap, perfumed whore — just one word — and I'll crash this fist of mine into your face so hard you'll think your damn throat's cut!" Larkin turned to the others, saying: "Now enough of this interference and being noble. Remember, I don't care what you think or what you say. I said I was goin' to brand my initials on the Midnight Lady's rump and that's what I'm going to do! Yes — and right now!"

A shocked silence followed his words; a silence of some ten seconds' duration, so tense it seemed to stand apart from time as though held there in a frame. Then as they stood there, wondering what would happen next, suddenly they all heard it. They heard that silvery laugh, then the chime-like voice which floated to them from the far end of that moonlight glen:

"But why harm the gypsy girl, Mr. Larkin, if you intend to brand the Midnight Lady? You see — I am over here!"

The entire assembly wheeled, their eyes going to the far end of the clearing.

There, an old wagon trail began to wind its way through the trees and towards the roadway, sixty yards away. And where it began, sitting on a coal-black horse and clearly revealed in the bright moonlight, was a masked woman whose wavy hair tumbled to her shoulders. To several of the raiders who had seen her galloping up and down main roads and side roads, there could be absolutely no doubt as to her identity. This was the Midnight Lady! The real Midnight Lady! That strange, galloping beauty, the mention of whose very name brought fear to their hearts. The magnificent beast she rode reared up with an impatient whinny, pranced briefly on its hind legs, then returned to all fours before she called out again:

"Your employer erred, Mr. Larkin, when he told you that Anita, the gypsy girl, was the Midnight Lady. However, it is but another of many mistakes he has been making lately, and each one only molds another nail for his coffin. Tell him that for me, but first, suppose you and I make a little wager?"

Having gotten over the shock of her surprising appearance, Dan Larkin was thinking — hard and fast. Yes, and one of the first thoughts to flash to his brain, was the fact that the real Midnight Lady sat on her horse, less than sixty yards from him. Just a hop, skip and a jump! Why if he was to make a sudden dash her way, bolt ahead and charge forward, he could have his hands upon her in five seconds, or six at the most; at least in lots of time before she would be able to wheel her horse and gallop off!

Yes, it was only a matter of getting her off guard then bounding forward. So Dan Larkin casually shuffled ahead as he readied himself for a dash.

Quietly he asked, "What kind of a wager are you talkin' about?" Anything to gain her attention.

Her answer was a motion of her right arm that was almost too quick for the eye to follow, and a revolver appeared in her hand. In the same instant it roared out smoke and flames, and the black hat of Dan Larkin was whisked off his head, to fall to the ground a dozen feet behind him.

"Don't try it, Mr. Larkin!" she spoke swiftly. "I am a champion shot, have many trophies to prove it, and could have put that bullet through your heart as easily as I put it through your hat. Try charging me, and I promise I'll have shot both your eyes out before you've gone six paces!"

She rose slightly in her stirrups and called out to the other raiders: "The same goes for you gentlemen, and for the sake of your loved ones I trust you believe me. I have two guns. You can all charge at once if you wish, but you have my word that the wife of any man who tries to rush me will soon be wearing crepe upon her bonnet!"

Involuntarily, the lot of them took a backward step. Fearless fist and club fighters they were, but they realized how slim their chances would be against a gun. Especially when it was held in the hand of the masked woman before them, a sample of whose uncanny marksmanship they had just witnessed. Raising her voice slightly, she spoke to the gypsies:

"You good people have nothing further to fear from these masked men. I know their names and if further harm befalls you, all of them will be seeing tomorrow's sunset behind bars in the London jail. Yes, and several thousand more sunsets to follow. Incidentally, you people remain in your present encampment and before two days have passed, you will be well compensated for this night's work."

To be sure they were, and the Midnight Lady must have had the riches of a score of kings. Two days later, around sundown, a distinguished-looking man with a legal air, drove up to the glen to deliver the cheque to Kibo that enabled him and his to live in modest comfort for many years. Yes, and while I think of it, a new violin was bought for Tony, who in later years made quite a name for himself in the world of music, just as one of his grandsons is doing in Hollywood today.

Having assured the gypsies of compensation, the Midnight Lady again turned her eyes to Dan Larkin.

"Now about that wager, Mr. Larkin," she began. "I understand you have said that you intend to brand your initials on the Midnight Lady, and just a few minutes ago I heard you say that the saddled horse beside you — Black Brook — is the fastest thing on four legs in these parts. Well, suppose we find out for sure!"

Once more that silvery laugh, and then:

"So here is what we will do. You mount Black Brook, and try to catch me. I'll give you an hour to do it and I promise not to use my guns. If you succeed, we will return to this camp and I will willingly submit to the branding iron." She paused, then added: "However, Mr. Larkin, if you fail to capture me at the end of that hour, we still return here but you must be branded by me. Not with my initials, but with a D.K. — across your face! Well, what do you say? Is it agreed?"

Just a dull, lifeless, "Huh?" came from Dan Larkin.

A moment of silence, then: "Well, Mr. Larkin, where is your sporting blood?" inquired the Midnight Lady.

Another silence, three minutes of it, this time, before a murmur of whispers came from the raiders. One of them called out: "All right, Dan; don't be like the little boy that messed his pants. Say something."

"In my opinion, the wager strikes me as being fair enough," spoke up another.

Dan Larkin wheeled to the second speaker, whose voice he recognized. "Keep your damn opinion to yourself, Tim Flynn!" he howled. "It's my face that's apt to get fried! Not yours!"

"Come, come, Mr. Larkin," called out the Midnight Lady. "Shouting at your followers is no way to act, and I am still waiting for your answer. I'm puzzled by not having heard it already, for surely the great and fearless Dan Larkin is not afraid? Not afraid to risk his skin in a race against a mere woman?"

Then she added: "Or is he?" And again she laughed.

That did it. It was said of Dan Larkin that he became a raging devil when angered — some even hinted that he went stark crazy — and the suggestion of cowardice on his part was enough to spur him to a frenzy of rage. Cursing a blue streak, he tore the handkerchief off his face, threw it on the ground, stamped it, then kicked it into the campfire, before he turned and shouted to the mounted one on the far side of the glen:

"Yes, I accept your challenge! You're damn right I do and I'll tell you somethin' else. I'm not only going to ride and chase you! I'm goin' to catch and bring you back here! Yes, and then I'll take my time and brand my initials as well as every other letter in the alphabet on you! On your rump, up and down your backside and on your face as well! Think that over — you slut!"

With that, Dan Larkin gave a wild shout and leaped upon Black Brook.

Across the glen, the Midnight Lady wheeled her horse and thundered up the winding wagon trail that led through the trees, while forty yards behind her, Black Brook streaked across the clearing to follow in hot pursuit. There came a series of thudding sounds as the two horses raced up the wagon trail, then the wild and loud clatter of hoofs which told the listeners that the riders had reached the hard surface of the main road. The furious din proclaimed that both horses were being forced to breakneck speed, and with such a terrible fate in store for the losing rider, it was quite understandable. Gradually, however, the sound subsided, became ever fainter and finally died away.

As for those remaining around the campfire?

When all was still once more, old Shena, Anita and Tony, gave aid to Kibo and his brother, while the gypsy youngsters returned to the wagons and slumber. One by one the eleven raiders removed their masks, then sat down around the campfire to stare steadily into the flames. And to wonder — to ponder — and to wait the outcome of that most hellish of all races!

CHAPTER THIRTEEN

The Night the Skeletons Rode

With torches blazing, they rode on,
And I once heard it said:
It seemed as though the graveyards had
All given up their dead.
— Old Song —

Once again the old man in the graveyard paused to
smile at the listening American couple. Then he went
on with his story.

At this point, he continued, you are probably anx-
ious to learn the outcome of that grim race between the
Midnight Lady and Dan Larkin. For my part, I am quite
ready to tell you, but before I do and while I think of
it, you might be interested in hearing a true story
regarding the Donnelly massacre, as well as hearing of
the whereabouts of the actual hatchet — still extant —
that was used to chop off Tom Donnelly's head.

Some day you may want to see it and want to learn
more about its strange and blood-curdling history. So
here it is.

First I would like to relate a bit of information
regarding Tom Donnelly. Undoubtedly the champion
scrapper of the Donnelly family, and a stern, quarrel-

some and hard man at best, Tom Donnelly did have —
despite the stories you might hear to the contrary — a
sweetheart. A young, hot-blooded Irish sweetheart. She
lived near the village of Lucan; she was a slender, brown-
haired and pretty maid named Christiana McIntyre, who
was destined to know many tears and heart-breaks in
the ninety-two years of life that were hers.

Her father, a farmer, was Murray McIntyre, once
well known in and around Lucan. She had a brother,
three years her senior, named Joseph. In the spring of
1878, when she first met Tom Donnelly, Christiana was
twenty. Tom was twenty-three.

Of course the fact that Tom was a Donnelly made
it impossible to hope that he could ever get the
approval of her family, nor did Christiana dare to be
seen with him in public. But love finds a way, and they
did manage to meet on a number of occasions, near an
old mill a mile from the village. These meetings
occurred about every two weeks and I am not saying
that anything went on; though it must be remembered
it was necessary that they meet at a secluded spot, and
they were young people and very much in love.

Then came the discovery. Christiana's horrified
parents learned that their daughter had been seeing a
Donnelly. The romance promptly came to an end, with
the girl being shipped off to London, where, the following year, she married a chemist and inventor
named Malcolm Wilson.

However, her brother Joe, never forgot that Tom
Donnelly had dared to court his sister, and on that
terrible night of February 4, 1880, Joe McIntyre was
not only one of the participants in the Donnelly massacre, it was his hand which wielded the hatchet that
chopped off Tom Donnelly's head.

Sixteen months later, in June 1881 when his home, along with that of the other Donnelly killers, was painted with a D.K., Joe McIntyre, unable to face the scorn of his neighbors, left the Lucan district and eventually secured employment in Ottawa and later in Montreal. Thirty-five years went by.

One day a gray-haired man of sixty, with suffering etched deeply on his features and fear in his eyes arrived in the village of Lucan. It was Joe McIntyre, returning home. He stayed there only a few days, then went on to London, where he remained for a long period at the home of his then widowed sister, Christiana, and her son, a minister, who lived on Carfrae Crescent. In secrecy, Joe McIntyre confided in his nephew — the minister — that he had been one of the Donnelly murderers; he also confessed he had chopped off Tom Donnelly's head with the hatchet he still had in his possession.

"For years I have lived in dread of old Johannah's prophecy," said Joe McIntyre. "As she was being clubbed to death, she shouted out that all the mobsters would die a violent death, and from what I have been able to find out, none of them — not a single one — has known a natural death. It has always been suicide, murder, or a strange or violent death."

With that, Joe McIntyre broke down and sobbed.

"Oh I'm still alive, even though the waters of thirty-five years have gone under the bridge since that damnable night; but it's been a living hell on earth for me, and I've seen old Johannah a thousand times in my dreams. She points an accusing finger at me and gives a terrible smile. Wherever I go it is always the same; she comes in the night to haunt me and I can't go on much longer!"

Joe McIntyre didn't "go on much longer." Less than two weeks after telling his story, his nephew found him in the shed behind the house, a rope around his neck, hanging from a beam. The nephew cut him down and kept the incident a secret. It was thought by all that Joe McIntyre was a victim of a heart attack. In later life the nephew settled in Vancouver and to his dying day he kept the hatchet once owned by his uncle. The hatchet that was used to chop off Tom Donnelly's head!

I forgot to tell you the identity of that nephew. Well, it seems that at the age of thirty-six he forsook the pulpit to turn to a life of crime, and became one of the few men in the history of crime to steal $16,000,000. His name was Herbert Emerson Wilson and he was once internationally known as the King of the Safecrackers.

Now let us go back to that grim race between the Midnight Lady and Dan Larkin.

Three hours after they had thundered out of the glen, Dan Larkin, dust-covered and travel-stained — minus his hat as well — began pounding on Cyrus Robbin's door shortly before four o'clock in the morning. On the roadway behind him, the horse, Black Brook — heavily lathered, steaming and breathing hard — was the picture of exhaustion and defeat, as he stood with tired legs and lowered head. Larkin continued to send a barrage of blows upon the door till it was finally opened by Cyrus Robbin, attired in nightgown and cap.

"So it's you — and about time!" began the Squire. "Connors rode over here two hours ago; he told me about the wager and the race. Well — well?" he asked.

Larkin snapped, "Well, what?"

"The Midnight Lady. You rode her down, of course. With a horse like that one beneath you, you could not fail. But what did you do with her? Where is the Midnight Lady?"

"Where is the Midnight Lady?" echoed the other, then shrugged and replied: "Well, if she's goin' as fast as she was when I had that last glimpse of her, she ought to be about half way to China by now!"

"What do you mean?"

"I mean it was all like some hellish nightmare!" exclaimed Dan Larkin. "To begin with, that horse of hers, I don't believe it is a horse; I think it is the devil himself disguised as a horse! Why there I was, mounted on Black Brook, a beast I could have sworn was the fastest in Canada, yet the fiend she rode was able to pull away from him as though he was tied to a post. As for the Midnight Lady! Why it was fun, it was all like some sort of game to her! She kept laughin' at me; as though she was chucklin' at some private joke of her own!"

The general summary of Larkin's story was that it had not been a race at all; just a mockery of one. According to him, from the very start the masked woman had made it most evident that her mount could run rings around his own, and she was only letting him stay fairly close to her so that the race would not be too lopsided. They galloped on for mile after mile; up one road and down another, while Dan Larkin beat and shouted at his horse. The Midnight Lady never touched hers.

Occasionally the Midnight Lady would give a sharp, shrill whistle, which would send her charger streaking ahead; increasing its lead to a hundred and sometimes two hundred yards. Other times she would deliberately pull in her horse and allow her pursuer to gain on her till he was scarcely two lengths away, as if she felt sorry for and sought to encourage him. This would go on for a bit, then, like a cat playing with a mouse, she would again give that sharp whistle, and once more her magnificent beast would bolt ahead as though shot from a giant bow, to practically double the speed of the lather-covered and tiring Black Brook!

"Why, do you know what she did once?" exclaimed Larkin. "We were two miles this side of Granton when I had to pull up to give my nag a breather, and what do you think? She rode back to me, shouted, 'Yes, rest awhile, Mr. Larkin. Both you and your horse need it!' And then — and may I be struck dead if I lie — she actually wheeled that tireless devil of hers, bolted up the road like a bat out of hell for a good quarter of a mile, turned around and shot back just as fast, to stop five yards from me and cry out: 'All right, Mr. Larkin; you've had your rest. Let's get started again!'"

"So I kicked Black Brook in the ribs, beat him hard across the rump with my fist and we were off once more! But it was like tryin' to race against greased lightnin'!"

"Where did the race end?" Cyrus Robbin wanted to know.

"Somewhere near Elginfield, when Black Brook couldn't go on. Just folded up and I had to dismount or he would have dropped beneath me. The Midnight Lady was a hundred yards in the lead at the time, but she turned, galloped back to me and said she was sorry the race had to end. Also said somethin' about havin' a grand night's entertainment. And that devil of a horse of hers — why it wasn't even breathin' hard. Before she left she called out:

"'As for the wager you woe me, Mr. Larkin, I may collect it someday. But to be really truthful, I think fate is going to collect if for me in some strange way of its own! Some terrible way!' Then she was off with the speed of a fallin' star — long cloak flutterin' behind her. As for me, I waited around till Black Brook got strength enough to get goin' again, and rode over here. Well, that's it!"

Cyrus Robbin shook his head. "No, Larkin; that's not it nor the half of it," was his reply. "Once word gets around to the D.K's that she beat you, it will only increase the seeming invincibility of the Midnight Lady and add to their panic. They will start to leave in droves."

Cyrus Robbin took a deep breath before he said: "Larkin, Larkin — I am afraid to think of what is ahead for us. One of those fools, those frightened rabbits, to gain the clemency of the Crown, is certain to talk; to tell what he knows and that means our ruination — maybe the noose!"

Cyrus Robbin wrung his soft white hands; fear came to his eyes as he said: "Yes, I'm worried! Very worried!"

Dan Larkin confessed: "With things goin' as they are, I can't say I feel much like dancin' a jig myself!"

A number of things happened the following week, which proclaimed the increasing fear of the remaining members of the mob.

To begin with, as Cyrus Robbin prophesied, some took to flight. In fact, during the following seven days no less than five D.K's — probably realizing the handwriting was on the wall — left the district and were seen no more. One, in order to get a cash sale, sold his farm for a fraction of its worth. When confronted with the fact, he is said to have answered, "Anything is better than nothing to get you to a place where you can wear a collar instead of a noose!"

A sixth Donnelly killer was also able to evade immediate justice during that week, though he did not resort to flight to do so. On Thursday night, that grim warning — a flaming torch — had been tossed before the gate of the home of Tim Flynn, the same Tim Flynn who had been in the glen with Larkin. The next morning when he failed to appear at the breakfast table after milking, Flynn's wife went to the cowshed to find her husband's body — his throat cut from ear to ear! His blood-smeared razor lay nearby! Maybe he thought it was the easiest way out!

The following Saturday William Donnelly was taking his daily buggy ride to Lucan, fiddle beside him, Paddy the crow perched on his shoulder, when he noticed a buggy coming his way with an occupant he had not seen in several years. A smile came to his face, for it was none other than the hundred-and-four-year-old Grandma Bell. For all her years, the aged woman, the district's noted teacup reader, milked her two cows twice daily, carried on with the household duties and thought nothing of driving to the village for her weekly supplies.

In passing, they pulled their horses to a halt, and William Donnelly called out: "Granny Bell — do you know me?"

"Know you?" came her reply. "Why I'd know your hide on a bush, Willie Donnelly, and only last night I was talking about you. Mrs. Monahon dropped in to see me, said she had heard you playin' your fiddle in Lucan a while back. I told her that I would have to drive over to your place sometime and soon, to hear you play once more. Of course you know who it was that gave you that fiddle of yours?"

He nodded and laughed. "I sure do, Granny. It was you, and it was exactly twenty-one years ago last January. I know, because it was my tenth birthday. I thanked you then; I thank you now."

A mere wisp of a woman, but wiry as they come, it was evident his answer pleased her.

"No need to thank me, Willie Donnelly," came her reply. "Your mother and father were always nice to me; I still think of them as two of the finest people I ever met. It is my own opinion that you Donnellys were blamed for many things you did not do, and as for the fiddle, well, it was only gathering dust around the house, anyhow."

He started to make some answer, when he noticed that a number of leaflets were fluttering around him and seemingly coming from above. Eyes raised, he learned that such was indeed the case, for several hundred pamphlets were turning and twisting as they descended from the blue, to finally reach the ground and go floating over the countryside. Yes, leaflets coming from the sky! But how — how — ? And then, way up in the blue overhead, William Donnelly suddenly saw something which brought a startled exclamation from his lips, and no wonder. He had just beheld his first balloon!

Now, since then, I have made it a point to read up on balloons, and learned that the first balloon ascension took place in France in June 1783. In the early 1840s, there were a number of balloon ascensions around Niagara Falls, which attracted thousands; but it is safe to say, even in 1881, that not one person in ten

— in the Lucan area — had ever seen one. And it was from the basket beneath the balloon that two people could be seen flinging leaflets which were deluging the district, sweeping downward like giant snowflakes. It was later estimated that five thousand leaflets float-ed downward, then the balloon finally vanished in the blueness of the east.

And the leaflets? In large, blue-black letters, they all had the same brief but direct-to-the-point message:

DONNELLY KILLERS!
This Is Your
Last Chance!
GET GOING BEFORE THE NOOSE GETS YOU!

That certainly commanded attention! And on that very Saturday night — while the remaining D.K's trem-bled in their boots — the Midnight Lady rode at the head of her skeleton army! She was really going all out for vengeance!

Around eleven o'clock that night fifty howling, mounted men — led by the Midnight Lady — rode over the Lucan countryside. All of them carried flam-ing torches. Each was dressed in black, tight-clinging garments and hoods, skillfully painted with the phos-phorescent glow that gave them a startlingly realistic, skeleton-like appearance. That bunch was enough to raise the hair on your head as they galloped along — the din of two hundred hoofs intermingling with their hoarse shouts that rose to the stars!

As agreed, and arriving from all directions so as to not attract undue attention by their number, they had met at a secluded spot, a mile or so from the old

Donnelly farm, where they were given their final instructions by the Midnight Lady. As I later learned, most of
them had been hired in nearby London — unem-
ployed men, capable of riding a horse, each of whom
received a handsome night's pay for their services. In
return, they had agreed to ask no questions when it
was learned that said services would actually break no
law, even if they did come mighty close to the border.

In secrecy, the horses were hired from a number of
surrounding livery stables.

Gad, what a sight it was, and even now, in memory,
I can still see it as plain as the night it happened! First
they made it a point to gallop past the homes of the
dwindling few D.K's that remained, at each house the
skeleton army would pull up to shout out three times
loudly: "Donnelly Killer, get out of the district!" Then
on they would ride to the home of the next — then the
next — then the next.

True, a few good folks who happened to be driving
back to their homes at a rather late hour, got the surprise of their lives and some might have known the
fright of their lives; but after all, it was for a good purpose and eggs have to be broken before you can fry
them. And while I think of it, there was a true and
mighty funny story told about that night which was
heard for many years to follow. It told of the two old
maids — the Quigley sisters — who were returning to
their house from a late visit to the outhouse, when
their eyes fell upon the approaching skeleton army. I'd
like to tell you the rest, but I guess it's a bit too off-
color to relate to mixed company.

Promptly at midnight, the Midnight Lady led her
galloping followers through sleeping Lucan, while the
air trembled with their wild shouts of "Donnelly

Killers, get out of the district!" Then on they rode till they reached the Roman Line, a mile away. It was somewhere near there they are said to have dispersed, riding in various directions as they made their way homeward after changing their clothes. It had certainly been a case of "there was a hot time in the old town that night!"

CHAPTER FOURTEEN

The Great Chase

They found him lying on the road,
In the dawn of that day.
Dead eyes looked skyward, but his soul
Had gone the other way.

— Old Song —

On the night of July 7, 1881, after several minutes of pacing his parlor floor in silence, Cyrus Robbin turned to Dan Larkin.

"All right, Larkin, suppose you begin again. You burst in here with a wild outflow of words about how you know you can catch the Midnight Lady without fail, then you speak so damn fast and crazy, that I can't make head nor tail of what you are talking about. Now first sit down, take a deep breath and count to ten, then start all over again. And go slow!"

Dan Larkin, a four days' growth of whiskers on his face and the smell of alcohol strong on his breath, pulled a chair forward and brought out his pipe, which he lit before he answered.

"You're jumpy as all hell tonight, Squire, but knowin' the lay of the land as I do, I can't say I blame you." He took several drags on his pipe, then said: "Of course you know that four more of the boys have left town during the last twelve days since the leaflets were dropped and the skeleton army rode?"

Larkin shook his head. "Just think, there are only ten D.K.'s left in this district. Ten out of the original thirty! The others are either dead or have vamoosed, and we've got to do somethin' about it."

Cyrus Robbin scowled as he seated his enormous bulk. "Did you come here to tell me that?" he asked. "I thought you had some plan for catching the Midnight Lady."

The other regarded him before he quietly spoke. "I have a plan that can only result in either one or two possible outcomes. I'll catch or kill the Midnight Lady!"

There was a shocked silence from the Squire before he exclaimed: "What? Kill? My God, man, you don't mean murder?"

Larkin nodded, "That's just what I do mean," then explained:

"We've already committed five murders, haven't we? Well, what's wrong with another one if it will save our necks? And before you get so squeamish," he went on, "you had better give some thought as to what would happen if you were dropped through a gallows. The weight of that big body of yours would pull your head from your shoulders! It would be real messy!"

Cyrus Robbin winced and gave a half sob, as he usually did at any mention of impending violence to himself.

Larkin explained his plan: First, by a letter, "given to William Donnelly, who, you can be damn sure, knows where the she-devil is," he would challenge the Midnight Lady to another race, with the wager being that he and the remaining Donnelly killers would leave the district if he failed to catch her. He said that she would be certain to accept the challenge; that she was too sure of herself, too confident, not to do so.

"This time, I'll have an ace up my sleeve; this time the race will be conducted as I want it," said Larkin, a smirk on his swarthy features. "And it will be the kind of race I love — a race where I can't lose."

He went on to confide that as well as the beast he would ride, he would have four other saddled horses waiting at various farms the racers were certain to pass, so the truth was — and Larkin chuckled — he would be riding five chargers against the lone mount of the Midnight Lady. "And I don't give a damn how good her horse is, it can't outrun five nags!" However, in the extremely remote event that it could, it would make absolutely no difference and mean only death to the masked woman. Because —.

"I've arranged for Mike Connors and Dan Shea to blast her to hell — blow her pants off!" exclaimed Larkin. "Neither of them is any hell as a marksman, but by usin' shotguns, they can't miss! They'll make mince-meat out of her!"

Cyrus Robbin encouraged him with, "Go on."

Larkin did: "Both Connors and Shea are desperate," he said. "Connors has six ragged kids, his house is damn near fallin' down; Shea's arse is out of his pants. I have them thinkin' the Midnight Lady practically has a noose around the neck of each of them; that she is a fiend from hell, that their only hope is to get rid of her. I hinted that such a deed would not only save their hides, but that you'd see they got a nice piece of money out of it as well. Oh, I was real clever about it. So we talked it over and it was agreed that for five hundred dollars apiece, they would be at the north end of the old Slattery farm with their shotguns. Right there by the road. Then, when I chase the Midnight Lady by them, they will riddle her to bits!"

And Dan Larkin exclaimed: "What do you think? Pretty clever idea, eh? Yes, and I figgered it out myself — right down to the last detail. Well?"

For some minutes Cyrus Robbin mulled over the plan in silence, while Larkin assured him that it could not fail. That nothing could go wrong; it was absolutely foolproof. Finally Robbin asked:

"This letter you are going to write to the Midnight Lady; how do you know William Donnelly will be able to get it to her?"

"Don't make me laugh and don't worry about that," answered Larkin with a knowing smile. "He knows where she is. Yes, and so do his brothers. Those three have been hand-in-hand with the Midnight Lady from the start, you can be plenty sure of that. Yes, I've only to give the letter to William Donnelly, and he will see that it gets into her hands."

"And you think she will go for your challenge?"

"With her thinkin' that me and the other Donnelly killers will leave the district if she wins? Of course she'll go for it — like a cat goes for liver!"

Cyrus Robbin wanted to know: "How about Connors and Shea? Can you rely on them?"

"Sure can, they'll do their part of the bargain; just give me the money to pay them off, they want it in advance," was Larkin's reply. "At the north end of the Slattery farm, right by the road, you know where that big rock is?" At the other's nod: "Well, that's where they will be waitin'. Then when she gallops by, with me chasin' her, two shotguns will go off — bang-bang! Yes, and that will be the end of the Midnight Lady!"

"By gad, Larkin, I hope so!" ejaculated Cyrus Robbin.

"Don't worry, it will be; it can't end any other way.
So let's have a drink on it, Squire — the Midnight Lady
is as good as dead!"

What followed? Well just before I tell you — went
on the old man — I would first like to make brief mention of a not-so-long-ago incident which occurred in
the Lucan area. In fact, though it happened in January
1962, it was directly connected with the Donnelly
feud, which supposedly terminated over eighty years
before. Yes, only that January, though nearly all of them
had been dead for many decades, it was because of
the Donnellys that the night skies of Lucan were once
more lit with flame! Why it was just like old times!

Of course there were other incidents shortly before
that; in 1961 a number of fires broke out in this district, whose origin was a mystery. Yes, it is quite true,
and recently I have heard several old-timers around
here say — in jest, of course — that the Black
Donnellys have probably returned from the grave and
are "up to their old tricks again — starting fires!" To be
sure, it was spoken only in jest but you know the old
saying: "Many a true word is spoken in jest."

Incredible, fantastic, you say, that fires of an
unknown origin should again be blazing in this district, like they did at the time of the Donnelly feud?
Well, first, let me refer you to the Toronto newspaper,
The Globe and Mail, whose issue of January 11, 1962
— page 23 — reports:

"London, Ontario. Jan 10: Eleven minor fires last
year at the village of Lucan, eighteen miles north of
here, were set, fire marshall's office inspector Robert
Kaufman of London said tonight. He said the fires are

still being investigated. He made the statement following the report of a twelfth fire, which last night burned down an old house used to store straw and hay."

Now for those who know the grim and bloody history of this once violent district, there are some sinister tales in connection with that "old house used to store straw and hay." Let me explain.

It is said that a group of men — beasts and devils, all of them — met at that old house to plan the atrocity which resulted in mutilating and cutting out the tongues of John Flannigan's stagecoach horses on the night of August 23, 1875 — a crime that was later blamed on the Donnellys. It is also rumored that other fiendish perpetrations were hatched there from time to time, which caused barns to be put to the torch, houses destroyed, a train derailed and cattle poisoned in the fields of surrounding farms. And it is known that on a July night in 1881, Mike Connors and Dan Shea met there, had several drinks, made last minute plans and inspected their shotguns before riding on to the old Slattery farm to kill the Midnight Lady!

Yes, it was an evil old house, associated with many terrible memories, and I for one was very pleased when it was finally destroyed. To be sure, it should have been done away with long ago. So that is why, on the night of January 9, 1962, that it was I, and I alone, who finally put the torch to that hell-house which had sheltered so many enemies of the Donnellys in bygone years!

Yes, and I am proud that I did it!

But now let me tell you of the great chase between the Midnight Lady and Dan Larkin. Needless to say, three nights after she received his letter, the two met at the site the missive had stipulated, near the Pat Kelly farm, some four miles north of Lucan.

It was nearly midnight, and as on their former meeting, again the night was clear, stars were gleaming and a full moon was in the sky, when Dan Larkin, riding a fast horse, drew near the Kelly farm and beheld the Midnight Lady. She was alone, mounted on her large black horse — and waiting. Several stiff drinks already warming his guts, a chuckle broke from Larkin's lips at the sight of her. Why she had ridden right into the trap! She had permitted him to approach her from the south, he had her just where he wanted her; and now had only to chase her before him like a sheep to a slaughter. There could be no escape; the rest was just a matter of time. He had only to wait till they rode by the Slattery farm! Realizing as much, a grin swept across the swarthy face of Dan Larkin; he rose in his stirrups to call out a harsh:

"Hello — you stupid bitch!"

Again that silvery laugh, like the jingle of distant sleighbells. And then once more he heard her musical voice: "Greetings, Mr. Larkin, nor do your words surprise me. After all, what can one expect from a pig — but a grunt? And now, shall we get started?"

"Have a good ride while you can!" he shouted. "It's the last you'll ever know!"

With that she turned the horse and galloped northward, while forty yards behind her, Larkin's horse followed in rapid pursuit.

For the first mile, there is not a great deal to be said. The Midnight Lady increased her lead to a hundred yards, seemed content with that distance and made no effort to widen it. Larkin, who carried a short whip, flicked it several times to the rump of his horse, but did not seriously try to overtake the one ahead of him.

Of course he had his reasons. So for some minutes both horses merely bounded along at a gallop, with neither being forced to a furious outburst of speed.

It was an even stretch of road which had been selected for that night ride. They passed occasional barns and farmhouses whose occupants were deep in sleep; once they both heard the sharp barking of an awakened dog, who reached the roadway just in time to snarl and snap at Larkin's horse as the beast galloped by. But the road was lonely and deserted for the first two miles of travel; at such an hour it was to be expected and there were no indications that it would be otherwise. But it was to be otherwise — Dan Larkin had planned well — and suddenly things began to happen!

Two and a half miles from where the race had started, the road took a sharp sweep eastward. And there two men were waiting with a fresh saddled horse.

Neither man made any attempt to halt the Midnight Lady. They had been instructed not to do so and had absolutely no intention of doing so. They had both heard of the uncanny marksmanship of the masked woman, realized she was probably armed and they wanted no part of her gunplay. So she was allowed to gallop past, but when Dan Larkin thundered up, ten seconds later, it was to swing from his hard-breathing horse, spring into the saddle of the one the men brought forward, and dash off once more.

Only now he rode a fresh mount, while the horse of the Midnight Lady had already galloped a rapid two-and-half miles!

This time Larkin beat his horse hard, right from the start, forcing it to its utmost speed as he sought to close the gap between him and the rider ahead. But for all his efforts, when a mile and a half more had been travelled, the Midnight Lady was still that tantalizing hundred yards ahead, nor did she appear to be even forcing that wonderful beast she rode.

He merely continued on and on with that seemingly tireless "Gallump-gallump-gallump," that gave every indication of never stopping till his beauteous mistress ordered it to. Several times she turned to cast a backward glance at her pursuer, and once gave the mocking hand-wave that brought a curse from Larkin.

Four miles from where the race had started, Dan Larkin's heart began to beat faster, for he realized that another horse — Black Brook, this time — was being held in waiting for him beneath an old elm, less than half-a-mile away, while a scant quarter of a mile beyond that tree, on the right side of the road, was the rail fence and large rock which marked the beginning of the Slattery farm — the large rock behind which Connors and Shea were waiting with ready shotguns. So, with loud curses, whiplashes and brutal kicks, Larkin forced his rapidly tiring horse to its utmost speed, while night winds whistled past his ears and dustclouds rose in the wake of his steed.

With the Midnight Lady riding on a hundred yards ahead of him, Larkin reached the elm tree. One of Cyrus Robbin's farmhands came forward with saddled Black Brook. Seven seconds later Larkin was in that saddle and riding off, but not before he had shouted out to the farmhand:

"Ride back to the Squire and tell him that the Midnight Lady is dead — a gone goslin'!"

Then he was on his way, while far in front of him the masked woman galloped towards the destruction that waited. On towards the start of the rail fence and the huge rock near the roadway, behind which, guns in hand, two Donnelly killers were ready for her coming — and made ready for her death!

Mike Connors and Dan Shea had arrived at the big rock a good half-hour before the Midnight Lady rode up to it.

Six paces to the left of them began the rail fence that marked the boundary of the old Slattery farm. Nearby was a thick, two-acre growth of bush; before them, their shotguns leaning against it, was a breast-high rock of four-feet width. Both of them were killers, desperately impoverished, and the money they had received for their scheduled night's work represented a fortune to them. Again, to their way of thinking, in getting rid of the masked woman they would have nothing more to fear from their part in the Donnelly massacre. As Mike Connors put it:

"Once we've blasted that Midnight Lady to hell, the past will be forgotten and we won't have to worry about it."

"Right," agreed the other. "The dead should be forgotten; she had no business coming here in the first place, raking up past dirt. She should have let sleeping dogs lie and she deserves what we're going to give her."

Connors said, "I'm sure going to give her plenty, and there won't be much of her left after she gets my fire. My gun's loaded with iron scraps!"

And Shea answered, "So's mine!"

The minutes passed as the evil pair waited; then shortly before one they both heard what they had been waiting for — the distant din of oncoming hoofs. It was warning enough; they exchanged knowing glances, sprang to their feet, reached for, grabbed and cocked their shotguns while the drumming hoofbeats came ever nearer. The next minute, in that clear moonlight, they could make out the approaching horse and its rider. It was the Midnight Lady, coming on fast; her long black cloak whipped out in the wind and streaming behind her. She was leaning slightly forward in her saddle, and they even caught the sparkle from the jewels on one hand: and, as they watched they saw her turn to give a backward glance at her pursuer.

Far behind her, Dan Larkin was being shot through the night on the fresh speedy Black Brook, his third mount.

Louder and louder came the hoofbeats. Suddenly the Midnight Lady was less than seventy yards away from them, rapidly drawing closer and —.

This was it, that terrible moment; yes, and both killers realized as much. This was what they had been paid for and they meant to earn their money. It mattered nothing to those heartless brutes that their victim was a beautiful woman, nor that the cause for which she struggled was honorable and just. No, that meant absolutely nothing; they thought only of their own welfare, their own rotten hides, and to hell with justice and honor. Yes, and after they had blown her to bloody shreds, they would go home, gut themselves, then sleep like pigs, without the slightest qualm of remorse. Just beasts — not men!

And so they took careful aim at that oncoming, glorious rider. The finger of each slowly tightened on the trigger of his gun. Nine — eight — seven — six — five! Only another five more seconds, now! Just five more seconds, and those damnable guns would blast out.

"Remember, when she passes us — let her have it!"

exclaimed Shea. And at the same time, from behind them, they heard a voice that roared out a commanding:

"Drop those guns, damn your souls, or we'll spread your guts all over the road!"

That did it! As one, both Shea and Connors were jerked erect by those words as if by invisible wires, as the shotguns slipped from their fingers and fell to the ground, while six feet before them the Midnight Lady and her charger swept by at a terrific speed, to go thundering loudly up the road and into the glow of the moonlight!

Ten seconds later Dan Larkin galloped by on Black Brook. He shot a puzzled glance towards the rock as he went past.

Then again came that commanding voice: "Turn around, you ugly freaks and face us — while your heads are still on your shoulders!"

Never in the history of the world was a command obeyed more promptly than that one. Dan Shea and Mike Connors spun around, and what they saw struck terror in their hearts. For standing less than six paces from then — armed with shotguns — were three grim and scowling men — William, Robert and Pat Donnelly! As usual, they were attired in rural work-clothes, and they looked plenty steamed-up, which was always a bad sign for their enemies. Then William spoke again; this time to Pat and Robert:

"Well, brothers, what should be do with the murderin' bastards who helped to kill our parents and brothers? Let's see, now. Will we blow their heads off; will we eagle-spread and stake them out on the ground, then start a fire on their bellies? Or should we be a little more polite, a bit refined-like, and just club them to death with the butts of our guns?"

Robert Donnelly snapped: "I'm for doin' all three of 'em!"

And Pat Donnelly snarled between clenched teeth: "Just let me get my hands on that damn Shea for two minutes, will you? I've always wanted to kick his arse till it bled!"

Pat dropped his gun and started to walk forward when William called out: "But Pat, you gave Shea a hell of a good beating four years ago! Remember?"

Pat Donnelly nodded as he advanced. "Yes, but it wasn't quite good enough to suit me. This time I'll give him an extra good beating, a real beauty, a darling, then I'll take on Connors and scramble up his ugly face!"

Mike Connors sank to one knee, fear in his eyes, as he extended a hand and implored: "Please, Pat, I've got six kids and —."

"You're a liar, you've got seven!" rasped Pat. "I know all about you and that Indian squaw who passed through here last year!"

William Donnelly gave a mirthless chuckle. "No, Pat I can't let you touch him, much as I'd like to," he spoke and reminded: "We gave our promise to the Midnight Lady that we would never use violence again and since she started running things for us, we have been getting along fine. Hell, we've been getting along perfect! Let's keep it that way!"

Then William Donnelly turned to Shea and Connors: "As for you skunks," he said, "I'd like nothing better than to take this shotgun, blow you both to hell and back, and then to hell again."

"Bill," broke in Robert Donnelly. "Suppose we take these two snakes to Lucan, and let folks know how they were going to shoot a woman — and for pay? You know what would happen, don't you, when word got around? They would be either torn to pieces or lynched by a mob. Maybe both!"

William Donnelly nodded. "I realize it and so do they, but we are going to do exactly as we promised the Midnight Lady." Then he said to Shea and Connors: "Now get this: It's her orders that you two are to ride home, pack your clothes and be out of this district by high noon. Tomorrow afternoon her lawyer — one of the many she has — will call upon your wives, buy your farms, give you a fair price for them and your families can join you later. But the pair of you must be out of here in eleven more hours. Now get going — and be damn thankful you're still alive!"

"Please, Bill, let me have Shea for just a minute, will you?" pleaded Pat. "I'd just love to pull out one of his arms and beat him over the head with the bloody end of it!"

But William Donnelly shook his head; neither he nor his brothers — true to their promise — as much as laid a hand on Connors or Shea, and that evil pair were allowed to ride away. As agreed — frightened three-quarters to death and shamed to the core as well — they left the district in a matter of hours, and their families later joined them. Shea moved to Ontario's Rideau Lakes district, and while winter fishing, three years later, the ice gave way and he was drowned less than a hundred yards from the old Monahon farm, near the small village of Newboro.

Two more years passed and Mike Connors, who had settled in the Niagara Falls district, celebrated his forty-fifth birthday by getting roaring drunk, then going to bed with his pipe still lit. It resulted in the burning and complete destruction of his small dwelling, and you could have put what was left of him in your hip pocket! From beyond the shade, old Johannah Donnelly must have chuckled. Her prophecy was still coming true!

But to return to the great chase: with Dan Larkin in fast pursuit, the Midnight Lady had galloped past the Slattery farm, then up the road that led away from it and into the moonlit night.

Behind her, Dan Larkin was a mighty bewildered man. What the hell had gone wrong? Why hadn't Connors and Shea killed the Midnight Lady when she rode by the big rock? He had seen neither them nor the Donnellys as he rode past; for a moment he could not understand why, and then between set jaws he snarled, "Those two stupid bastards probably got drunk and fell asleep beside the rock!" His eyes went to the rider ahead of him as he thought:

"It's up to me now! I have to catch her; I've got to — or it means my neck!"

Under ordinary circumstances, his chances of catching her would have been excellent. By then both racers had covered a good five miles, but Larkin was now on his third mount, the fresh and speedy Black Brook, while the Midnight Lady's horse had run the whole five miles. Ah, but that was just it; that was the catch, thought Larkin. That damn horse she rode was not a horse at all; not a thing of flesh and blood that would finally get winded, leg-weary and slow-up. No, it was a devil, that's what it was; a faster-than-the-wind and tireless, bounding devil, that could gallop on and on from here to hell and back, and not even breathe hard!

And yet — he had to catch the Midnight Lady!

So Dan Larkin forced the swift Black Brook to his utmost speed for the following mile, and then made a pleasing discovery; one that slowly brought a smile to his lips as he fully comprehended it. Why — why he was gaining! Yes, he was actually gaining fast on the Midnight Lady, whose charger seemed to have reached the end of its strength and was rapidly tiring. The hundred yards lead had been cut to fifty — then to forty — then thirty! Dan Larkin could hardly believe his eyes, and as he continued to draw even closer — and the masked woman was finally just a little more than three horse lengths away — a wild triumph suddenly swept over Larkin. Exhalted, he shouted out:

"I'll get you! In another two minutes I'll have my hands on you — and then I'll wring your damn neck!"

He heard that jingling laughter as she turned in her saddle to call out: "I'm afraid you misunderstood, Mr. Larkin. I have purposely let you catch up to me that I might make a suggestion."

"Huh? What suggestion?"

"I'm sure you will like it."

"Well, what is it?"

"That we stop this silly going along at a snail's pace, and that both of us show some speed! Come on, Mr. Larkin," she cried out, "let's see how fast our horses can really go! Yes, and I'll give you a hundred thousand dollars in cash if you can even keep me in sight!"

Once more her laughter and then again he heard it — that sharp, silvery whistle she had employed during their former chase, Ah, and that did it! And by the horns of the devil, how that did it! For no sooner had that shrill whistle stabbed through the night, than a wild surge shot through the beast she rode, and it bolted ahead like an eagle in flight. With a speed almost impossible to believe, it tore along the road, on and on, like a runaway engine roaring down a mountainside, as it left Dan Larkin and the laboring Black Brook far in its wake. Then farther — farther — and still farther — to finally disappear from Larkin's view!

Then it all came to him. Realizing how the Midnight Lady had duped him — led him on, laughed at and made a fool of him — Dan Larkin's short temper broke, and he threw back his head and emitted a loud, wolf-like howl of rage that rose to the stars! It was followed by a long string of vile curses.

What exactly happened to Dan Larkin after the Midnight Lady disappeared from view we will probably never know although a few facts are known.

With the dawn, two farmers driving a light cart into Lucan for supplies found him lying near the Foley farm on that lumpy stretch of sideroad that runs by the house. Nearby in mute misery, a broken foreleg raised, was Black Brook who was later destroyed. There was enough evidence to conclude that the horse, being forced to a terrific speed, had stepped into a deep rut and plunged forward on its face, while its rider had gone sailing over its head, to break his neck in the ensuing fall. Larkin lay full-length on his back in the centre of the road; his dead face, jaw dropped, looked upward with sightless eyes!

Thus died Dan Larkin, thief, sadist, brawler and murderer; and the more I think of it, the more I am inclined to believe that there might be some truth in the words of that old song which tells of him:

They found him lying on the road,
In the dawn of that new day.
Dead eyes looked skyward, but his soul
Had gone the other way.

CHAPTER FIFTEEN

Death Comes to a Monster

In terror that fat fiend ran on,
But no shelter could he find,
Nor was he able to escape,
That charging brute behind.

— Old Song —

Shortly before four in the morning of the fifth day after the death of Dan Larkin, the three Donnelly brothers William, Robert and Pat — in answer to a message from the Midnight Lady — rode their horses through the opened gateway that led to a large partly-wooded field, two miles south of Lucan. And under a nearby tree, in the ghostly glow of a pre-dawn light, stood the Midnight Lady. Beside her was her invincible, coal-black horse, that magnificent charger, whose fantastic speed and endurance had become a legend.

The masked woman motioned the Donnellys toward her.

"Greetings, good friends," she began, "and though it pains me to say it, this is destined to be our last meeting. You see," she explained, "my work here is completed; or at least it will be in a very few minutes. And then I must say goodbye and return, back to my home and my thousands of broad acres in a sunny, distant land, for the Donnellys will have been avenged!"

They came forward and dismounted and sat down on a log while she sat on another.

"I am expecting a visitor soon, but before he arrives I will enlighten you brothers on several matters that may still be somewhat of a mystery," she began. Then her eyes went to the pet crow on William Donnelly's shoulder; she called out a friendly, "Hello, Paddy," and went on:

"You will recall the night we first met, when I rode up to your house as your kitchen clock was striking midnight to announce the beginning of February 4, 1881?" At their nod: "At that time I told you I would bring around the downfall of your enemies without the slightest physical violence, nor would it be necessary for you to strike a single blow in retaliation. Well, it has all happened as I told you it would, but you will remember I also said that my campaign would make it necessary to play upon the superstition and fear of the surrounding countryside. They had to be terrorized; the innocent as well as the Donnelly killers. There was no other way."

William Donnelly nodded as he spoke up. "Yes, we remember."

"Then, first let me tell you that the story told by the elderly Mr. and Mrs. Michael Ryan — how your parents and brothers returned from the grave and called upon them — was entirely fictitious and told at my request. I knew such a story would create panic; I also realized it would be believed by practically the entire district if told by the Ryans who are known for their honesty and have been for years. They were the ideal pair."

"Again, the Ryans were wretchedly poor," she pointed out. "So when I told them that such a story would not only frighten the Donnelly killers and help the cause of justice, but that I would enrich them as well for their narrating it, they agreed. It was, they realized, for the best interest of the community. Later, at my request and for a certain sum I paid them, the Quigley sisters told a similar tale, which brought more fear to the Donnelly killers."

Pat Donnelly started to speak but she raised a hand for silence and went on:

"There were, of course, a series of strange happenings, some of them fantastic, that cannot be explained. To be sure, the balloon that scattered the pamphlets, as well as the ride of the skeleton army, was all arranged with my money; but the violent deaths of Dan Dunn, Barney Harrigan and the others —" She paused and shrugged her graceful shoulders.

"They are matters that cannot be explained," she said. "Maybe they were all but a strange series of coincidences; maybe there is some truth to that final curse of Johannah Donnelly. I do not know."

From the grayness of the pre-dawn light in the south, came the distant din of rumbling buggy wheels. The Midnight Lady rose from the log where she had been seated and said:

"However, I do know who will be in that oncoming buggy, and must ask that none of you speak or take part in what is about to happen. You are to remain silent; to be witnesses and nothing more. What will shortly occur is a settlement that concerns only us, and can be concluded only between the approaching driver and myself!"

As she spoke, the buggy drew ever nearer, then

became visible in the thin grayness of the early dawn.
A team of bays drew the buggy; sleek, fast-stepping
animals well known throughout the district. Then, as a
wandering breeze swirled up a dust cloud on the road
before them, the horses were pulled to a stop directly
in front of the opening gateway. The driver, meticulously dressed, descended from the buggy, and gazed
around them before walking pompously forward.

It was Mr. Cyrus Robbin!

Six paces from the Midnight Lady, Cyrus Robbin
halted, to purr in his soft, feminine voice: "I believe it
was you who sent me the letter requesting my presence here at this most ungodly hour?"

"Come now, Mr. Robbin," was her amused answer.
"I did not request your presence here; I demanded it!
You know that!"

Cyrus Robbin stole a glance at the three seated
Donnelly brothers before his gaze went again to the
Midnight Lady. She wore dark riding boots and
breeches, as well as a black satin shirt, open at the neck.
And, of course, her long cloak. A dark lace mask was
secured at the back of her head; wavy, blue-black hair
fell to her shoulders. Then Cyrus Robbin exclaimed:

"That letter you wrote me. Ridiculous! The crime
you charge me with. Preposterous!"

He drew himself erect and half raised a clenched
hand in the manner of one outraged. But the Midnight
Lady only shook her head to answer quietly:

"No, Mr. Robbin; the letter was not ridiculous, the
charge not preposterous. It is true, you know it; the
very fact you are here now only proves as much!"

She went on. "However, in the event you think I
might be unable to prove my charge, I would like to

remind you that it would be a very simple matter to have the body of your victim exhumed in the presence of police authorities, and find the evidence of arsenic poisoning that will still be there. Oh yes, it will be there, even after seven years. Then, to remove all doubt, there is the confession of Allen Thomas —"

"What? You know of Allen Thomas?"

"I know a bit about him, Mr. Robbin; certainly all that is necessary to know. I also have in my possession his written confession, penned in Buffalo seven months ago in the presence of my lawyers, only two days before his death. It explains everything in detail, I promise you. The entire story. Now tell me, are you so stupid and so very, very cowardly that you still deny your guilt?"

At first he had gasped; then Cyrus Robbin's three hundred pounds began to tremble before her words. He opened his mouth to make some reply, thought better of it; removed his hat, pulled a handkerchief from his hip pocket and wiped his forehead though the early morning was quite cool. Finally, in a barely audible voice, he half sobbed:

"Your words — they cut me cruelly — so cruelly! Nor is it fair as I am a kindly man at heart. And — and I was not myself — not myself at all at the time it happened!" Raising eyes skyward as though appealing to the Almighty, Cyrus Robbin wailed out: "Did mortal man ever suffer as this woman is making me suffer now?"

He sank to his knees, buried his head in his arms and wept!

With Robbin's sobs resounding behind her, the Midnight Lady turned to the three Donnelly brothers.

"On the occasion of our first meeting, I said I would one day tell you the name of the man who actually brought about the massacre of your parents and brothers. I told you the members of the mob who perpetrated the murders were only puppets, the dupes and hirelings of one man. They were deceived by his lies, obeying his orders without question, as most of them were indebted to him in one way or another. But he and he alone was the real destroyer of your kin, and now that fat hypocrite sobs before you! Mr. Cyrus Robbin!"

And Cyrus Robbin, still kneeling, raised his eyes as he beseeched the remaining Donnellys: "Please — please — I am sorry — so sorry!"

That did it; that was it! On his knees, the instigator of that bloody massacre was begging forgiveness. I said that the vengeance of the Black Donnellys was at last a fact! Triumph! They had won!

Yet as though she had not heard the words, the Midnight Lady went on: "But why, you brothers are asking yourselves, why did Cyrus Robbin hate the Donnellys so much that he wanted to destroy them?" A little laugh escaped her. "Ah, it is a story as old as the hills themselves, though in this case the ending was somewhat different. So let me explain:

"It began back in the early spring of 1874 when Cyrus Robbin, then nearing fifty, first met your beautiful sister, Jennie, who was eighteen at the time. Of course Cyrus Robbin was married but he had never loved his wealthy wife. Then he met lovely Jennie, and for the first time in his life his heart beat faster. The girl's beauty and freshness practically drove him to the verge of madness, though she was innocently unaware of the fact.

"Of course he was as monstrous and repulsive then as he is now — married as well — and realized how hopeless his feelings were; knew she was hardly aware of his existence. But he frequently drove by the Donnelly farm, hoping to see her, in the yard and fields. He got to know her schedule for driving into the village, and always made it a point to be on the road, so they could meet and exchange a few casual remarks — he acting and talking in a friendly, fatherly manner, when all the while his evil heart ached to crush her to him.

"Then Cyrus Robbin came to a decision. He would do away with his wife, hoping, that, when free, his money and position, might make him an eligible suitor.

"The less said about how he murdered his wife the better; so I will only say that with the aid of one of his farmhands, Allen Thomas, who, for a price, obtained the arsenic, Cyrus Robbin poisoned his wife. He was not suspected; her death was attributed to heart failure. Then a terrible surprise awaited him. A few weeks after her death, he arranged it so that he would meet Jennie Donnelly as she drove into Lucan for supplies. He stopped her buggy, told her he loved her and asked her to marry him. To his amazement, pretty Jennie Donnelly laughed at him.

"'You must be mad, Mr. Robbin!' she cried. 'Why you are old enough to be my father! And you are hardly my idea of a dream prince!' Again she laughed.

"The following month, Jennie Donnelly, visiting relatives in St. Thomas, met the young man who won her heart. An ideal couple, they married a short while later.

"Overnight Cyrus Robbin became a veritable devil. He could not forget that Jennie Donnelly had laughed at him. His former infatuation turned to a terrible hate, as he sought to make her suffer in the only way he could — by striking back at her family. A number of fires in this district, deliberately started by Robbin and his men, were blamed on the Donnellys. So were other outrages — poisoned cattle, mutilated horses and other vandalism. Lies, lies and more lies were told about the Donnellys — at Robbin's orders. The years passed, but his hatred for the family so increased that it became a sort of madness with him. Then finally, with lies, money and promises, he was able to bring about the now notorious Donnelly massacre, though he took no part in the actual killings.

"And all because a pretty girl had laughed at and refused to marry him.

"I learned all this from my investigators, who were finally able to find Cyrus Robbin's former farmhand, Allen Thomas, who, destitute and dying of consumption, was eking out a miserable existence near Buffalo. Aware of his approaching death, Allen Thomas confessed his part in the crime and later wrote a full confession, naming Cyrus Robbin as the actual murderer of Julia Robbin. Well, that is the story, and now you know, William, Robert and Patrick Donnelly, why your parents and brothers were murdered, as well as the identity of the one who caused their massacre!"

The Midnight Lady wheeled, pointed an accusing finger at Cyrus Robbin and snapped:

"And now you must pay! The hour is at hand! You must pay, not only for what you have done to the Donnelly brothers, but also for what you have done to me!"

Cyrus Robbin had risen to his feet while she told

her story. At her threat he took three steps backward, terror in his eyes. He seemed hardly able to force out the words:

"What — what are you going to do? I can't stand pain!"

"First I am going to tell you why two of your murderers — Mike Connors and Dan Shea — were unable to shoot me that night from behind the big rock at the Slattery farm," came her firm reply. "You see, Cyrus Robbin, you and Dan Larkin were overheard as you planned to kill me by an employee of mine who informed me of the plot. I, in turn, told the Donnelly brothers who took care of Connors and Shea. It was that same employee of mine who also informed me, from time to time, of a number of other plans of yours, and always well enough in advance for me to ruin them."

There came Cyrus Robbin's hollow voice. "That accomplice, that employee of yours — who is he?

"One of your farmhands," was her answer. "He also works for me — I pay him exactly ten times what you do — and he was a great one for listening outside your half-opened window, and seeing that the news got to me quickly. I am referring to that free drinking, wizened and lovable little Irishman, Danny Doyle. He has been a great help to me."

Then one hand shot inside her cape and came out in the next instant with a revolver!

While the Donnellys looked on, the Midnight Lady continued. "Now heed me well, for I will not repeat my words. I am going to give you a fifty-fifty chance to save your life. In that cluster of trees you can see to the right, is a bull, brought here from one of my herds, huge and powerful, that was originally intended for the bullring in Mexico City. Now, as any authority on fighting bulls will tell you, they are unpredictable; no one can say for sure what they will do next. In your case, Cyrus Robbin, I would say you pray that the one among the trees continues to doze as he is doing now!"

She gestured towards the fence at the far end of the field — at least five hundred yards away — and ordered:

"Start running for that fence you disgusting monster, for your very life depends on your fleetness of foot. If you reach the fence and scramble over it before you are overtaken, you are safe. For my part, I will wait till you have advanced a hundred yards into the field; then I will fire this revolver once — just once and then we will all see what will happen!"

Once more that silvery laugh rang out before she added:

"I would say, from here on you are in the hands of fate. That bull among the trees may continue to doze on; or, again, startled by my gun-shot, he might come charging forth, wild and destructive! As I said, a fighting bull is unpredictable. I do know you have at least a fifty-fifty chance of survival — certainly a far greater chance than you gave your murdered wife or the massacred Donnellys!"

And then, her voice loud and clear, the Midnight Lady cried out:

"Now run, even though the weight of the murdered must hang on you like heavy anchors! Run; it is your lone chance for survival, so make for the distant fence with a speed you have never equaled before! Yes, run, Cyrus Robbin! Run for your life!"

And that great coward, Cyrus Robbin?
What did he do, the swine who had brought about

the massacre of the Donnellys? What did he do, that fat and loathsome brute, whose maniacal jealousy through the years had caused the outrages and tragedies in this district? Ah, I will tell you what he did and it was typical of him. At first he made as though to fall to his knees, to sob and beg for mercy. But he must have known that any plea for mercy would be useless. Wasted. Utterly futile. And then, perhaps, the thought flashed to his brain that his one hope was flight. Immediate flight! Fast and furious flight! For suddenly —

Suddenly, with a high, child-like wail, Cyrus Robbin wheeled and began what was — for a man of his weight — an amazingly fast and bounding dash across the field, as fear lent wings to his heels.

Behind him the Midnight Lady waited till he had advanced some distance before she raised and fired her revolver into the air. Only one shot, just one shot — but it was enough!

The next minute, amid a sharp crackling of twigs and branches from the trees and into the open plunged an enormous coal-black bull, whose long pointed horns resembled deadly rapiers. Almost immediately his eyes fell upon the running Cyrus Robbin, eighty yards away, and for several seconds the brute regarded the winded and laboring man. A massive hoof pawed the ground, the earth shot up as though thrown from a shovel. And then, with lowered head and a fearsome bellow that would have quailed the heart of a Spartan — the great monster charged!

It was soon over!

Running with a speed made possible only when terror is the pacemaker, and shrieking at the top of his voice as he did so, Cyrus Robbin sought to keep a distance between himself and destruction; but the race was hopeless. While still a hundred yards from the fence he sought to reach, the man who had master-minded the massacre of the Donnellys was overtaken, tossed high, tossed high again, then gored, gored repeatedly, crushed and trampled upon. When the great bull finally tired of its sport and returned to the cluster of trees it had left, Cyrus Robbin — a mass of gory flesh and practically every bone in his body bro-ken — truly resembled the proverbial "something the cat dragged in!"

Death had come to a monster!

CHAPTER SIXTEEN

I Loved a Wild Irshman

And as the sun rose up that day,
She waved to the Donnelly men.
Then the Midnight Lady rode away,
And was never seen again.
— Old Song —

"The scene you just witnessed, at long last writes the final chapter to the thirty-three year Donnelly feud and proclaims — with the terrible fate of Cyrus Robbin — that justice has triumphed and the Donnellys have finally won!"

The Midnight Lady spoke the words to William, Robert and Pat Donnelly, less than a minute after the death of Cyrus Robbin, adding:

"And now there are but five Donnelly killers left in the Lucan district, since the other twenty-five have either come to some terrible fate or fled to parts unknown. As for the remaining five, it is not necessary that we think of them; they played only minor roles in the massacre, were insignificant spectators rather than killers. Again, their identity is known to many, and each must face the scorn of the community in the years ahead as well as live with their own conscience.

Also, they dwell in constant fear of Johannah Donnelly's curse, wondering if, like so many other Donnelly killers, they too will eventually die a violent death and in just what manner it will come to them!"

Then she said: "Yes, it is all over now; the time has come for me to say good bye." And for the first and only time there was a faintest tremor in that wondrous voice. Around her was the beauty of a golden dawn.

William Donnelly broke a long silence to speak up: "Please, and I speak for my two brothers here as well as myself when I say it, we want to thank you for what you have done. Oh I realize thanks is little enough, but it is about all we have to offer."

"Not quite!" put in the impulsive Pat Donnelly. "From now on you can always count on us," he told the Midnight Lady. "Yes, and if any man ever as much as harms a hair on your head, I'll feed his gizzard to a lizard!"

"Thank you, Patrick," came her amused answer. "It is nice to know that I can always depend on you Donnelly boys."

And with Paddy the crow clinging to his shoulder, William Donnelly spoke again: "However, young lady, you did promise that one day you would tell us why ...." His voice trailed off.

She motioned them to seat themselves again on the nearby log, and said: "And the best part of it all is that at no time did you Donnellys have to resort to violence or lawlessness to gain your victory. It was brought about by your shrewdness, clever planning, cunning and foresight — and perhaps a wee bit of help from me."

Then, seated, the Midnight Lady let her gaze roam over the broad field to the left of her; next she looked at her horse, who came forward till he stood directly behind her — proud and magnificent. Finally, her eyes returned to the Donnellys as, leaning forward, she began her story:

"First," she said, "there are three surprising facts about me that you must know. Number one is that I am black, or at least there is black blood in my veins and I am proud of it. Number two is that you have known my great grandmother all your lives, for she is none other than old Granny Bell, the teacup reader who has lived in this district for well over four-score years. And the third fact; perhaps the most surprising one?

"I was once loved by and loved a wild Irishman! The murdered John Donnelly — your brother!

"But first," she went on, "let us go back nearly sixty years, when my grandmother — Granny Bell's daughter — left this district and travelled to Windsor, just across the river from Detroit, to work as a domestic. There she met and married a young Mexican; several years later, with his wife and a small daughter, he returned to his homeland. Around 1838 that 'small daughter' had become a pretty girl of twenty, who married an American prospector who in later years stumbled upon a fabulous silver mine in Montana. Eventually becoming enormously wealthy, the couple returned to Mexico where their daughter — my mother — married a Spanish nobleman, uniting two massive fortunes.

"And in one of their summer homes, a great castle on a high cliff overlooking the Pacific near San Blas, Mexico, I was born twenty-three years ago.

"Educated in private schools in the New World and later the Old, I must have been the despair of my mother who looked forward to my becoming a socialite. However, since childhood I have had only two loves: guns and horses. In time I mastered both. Countless hours of galloping over the broad plains of one of our ranches taught me the finer points of riding, while constant practice with firearms made my marksmanship close to perfect, and won me a number of trophies.

"Then, when I was twenty-one and studying in Italy, I was called home because of the tragic death of my parents. Inheriting their huge fortune I became one of the world's richest people. The following year I decided to journey to Canada and visit the great-great-grandmother I had never seen. She had lived more than a century, but as you are aware, was none too well fixed with worldly goods. She is an independent and proud old lady, and always refused financial aid from my parents.

"I arrived at Granny's cottage on a snowy day in late December in 1879; that same night your brother, John Donnelly, happened to call to see her. As I soon learned, Granny Bell and you Donnellys were always on good terms; John's friendly visit was but another of many he had made in the past. Of course I arrived alone and with my identity a secret to all but Granny, since we both realized the public attention my visit would cause her if it became known that I was not only her great-great-granddaughter but also the richest woman in the world.

"I had been literally showered with masculine attention since I was sixteen and had received, in my homeland as well as America and abroad, numerous proposals of marriage; some from honorable and wealthy young men of blue-blood families, along with others not so honorable or wealthy fortune-hunters, impoverished nobles and even a dissipated ex-king of a small European country, but I had never met any man who ever remotely interested me. I never expected to.

"Then, on that snowy December night in 1879, while wild winds wailed over and around the house and icicles hung from its roof, John Donnelly walked in, and from the first time we looked into each other's eyes I knew love!

"But I must be brief, for the dawn is upon us. Suffice to say that John Donnelly became a steady visitor at Granny's. Soon he asked me to marry him. Of course he knew nothing of my wealth; I decided to surprise him with that news later. I said I was employed as a domestic in Detroit and he believed me. When declaring his love and asking me to be his wife, I reminded him of my black blood. But my wild young Irishman only threw back his head and laughed:

"'Sure then, we'll be able to raise stalwart, fightin' sons, who'll carry a shillelagh in one hand and a razor in the other!' He laughed again and said: "'As to that what-you-are business, me darlin', how do we know that a hundred million years ago, the ancestors of all of us might not have been swingin' by their tails from the trees in Africa? Sure, an' the only difference is that my ancestors may have left the country before yours did, and maybe they had to. The others probably ran them out for gettin' drunk on fermented coconut juice!'

"'But John,' I pointed out at his insistence I marry him, 'what will we do for money?'

"'I told you I can get a high payin' job as a teamster in Detroit — and at two dollars a day!' he reminded me. 'Besides, I've three hundred silver dollars hidden in the haymow, so we've nothing to worry about for a long time. We'll live like kings!' Then he pointed to the ring I had neglected to remove. 'And there will be no more wearin' that cheap piece of green glass, darlin'!' he exclaimed. 'I'll get my wife a fine diamond ring, so I will, even if it costs as much as fifty dollars!'

"So I removed 'that cheap piece of green glass.' A massive and sparkling emerald once worn by a Spanish queen and worth a fortune.

"It was finally agreed that early on Wednesday, February 4, 1880, he would ride over the Granny's, where we would take a cutter, drive to London, catch the early morning train to Windsor and be married in the border city. And he finally agreed to my request; to tell no one of either myself or our intentions until after we were wed. Well, you can probably guess the rest.

"At 4 a.m. on that terrible Wednesday morning, Granny and I were up, my grips were packed, wood was crackling in the stove and preparations were being made for breakfast, when we heard the loudly shouted, 'Hello, in there!' that came from the roadway. We both hurried to the door; outside all was black and cold. And there on the roadway, holding their lanterns, were two riders whose purpose it was to inform the countryside of the great tragedy.

"I noticed a terrible blood-red glow in the far-away black of the winter sky.

"'Granny Bell, have you heard it? My God, it's terrible!' yelled out one of the men. 'A mob of thirty or so maniacs have just wiped out the Donnellys! Massacred — mutilated — clubbed them to death and burned down the blood-splashed house over their dead bodies! See — there's the glow of the flames in the sky!'

"'Yes; but that's not all!' roared the other. 'After they slaughtered the four Donnellys in the house —'

Granny cupped her ear.

"'I said, after the mob slaughtered the four Donnellys that were in old Jim's house, they walked the three miles to William's home to kill club-footed Billy. When they got there, a trio of them sneaked forward, knocked on the door and when it was finally opened, fired three shotguns full in the face of the one that opened it!'

"'But it wasn't William Donnelly, the one the mob wanted!' shouted the first. 'All dressed and evidently just about ready to leave the house and go somewhere — it was John Donnelly! The three shotguns blew off his head and tore John Donnelly to bloody bits!'

"Then the riders thundered off to spread their terrible news over the countryside! News soon destined to horrify North America in the screaming headlines of a hundred papers!

"From that hour I lived only for vengeance. Heavily veiled, I was in the church the day of the funeral services and slipped a letter into your coat pocket which you later found. Then I returned to my homeland to carefully plan my campaign to bring about the downfall of those who had murdered my beloved, along with his parents, brother and niece. I sensed that it had not been done with the common consent and wish of that mob of murderers. It was my opinion that there was a clever mind behind it all, who, for some unknown reason, brought about that massacre.

"Sparing neither time nor expense, I hired a number of the best private detectives in the country. Each had his specific orders; some of them passed themselves off as wandering farmhands, obtained employment on surrounding farms and kept their ears open. Two of them, for certain periods of time, actually worked for Cyrus Robbin. Then, at the end of the year, I had learned all that I needed to know — including the identity of every member of the mob that had murdered the Donnellys.

"There is little more to tell; the three of you know what followed. Our planning. Our night rides. Our final victory. I just want to say again that victory was brought about without the slightest lawlessness or violence on your part. You refrained from using force or brute strength; you kept your promises to me. I am very proud of you.

"Yes, and I only wish fate had willed that the three of you had become my brothers-in-law. I could have asked for no greater honor. And that, in conclusion, is my opinion of the Donnellys of Lucan!"

Her story over, the Midnight Lady rose to her feet, tall and shapely in the glow of dawn — her tapering fingers, diamond adorned, terminated by pearl-like nails. Behind her the great black horse gave a little neigh and pushed his nose forward on her shoulder for attention.

"Pegasus," she told the brothers. "Champion of champions and pride of Mexico, where he was born on a ranch of mine near Satillo. He was named after the winged horse of mythology, and I have been told by men who should know that a beast such as Pegasus is sired about once a century. I had him shipped here as I knew I would have need for him, and never for an instant did he fail me."

Around them the world was waking to a new day. A fresh crispness in the air mingled with the aroma of dew-drenched grass and growing fruit from a nearby orchard. The first chirping of the birds had begun; in the blue overhead several starlings winged across the sky as the faint crowing of a rooster came from a distant barnyard. In silence the Midnight Lady walked from the trees to the opened gateway which led to the road, followed by the Donnellys and the incredible Pegasus, "champion of champions."

William, Pat and Robert Donnelly suddenly felt a strange ever-mounting sadness; one which tugged heavier and heavier at their hearts, as realization came that this wondrous masked woman — and truly their "champion of champions" — was about to walk out of their lives. Forever. For the first time they fully understood how much they owed her, how much they depended upon, needed and looked to her for guidance. Why without her they would be nowhere! And now — They realized they would never see her again! Never!

They reached the roadway in silence.

Then, with one foot in the stirrup and about to swing into her saddle, the Midnight Lady halted when William Donnelly asked her for a token, some keepsake he might carry to remember her in the years ahead. She paused, regarded him for a minute, then reached into a pocket of her riding breeches and produced a twenty-dollar gold piece which she asked to be flung far aloft — way up into the blue. He did just that with a powerful throw; and as it shot heavenward the Midnight Lady whipped out her revolver — and believe it or not — put a bullet hole, dead centre, through that twenty-dollar gold piece!

For the last time they heard that silvery laugh, before she called out: "There, William Donnelly! You can think of me every time you look at it!"

William Donnelly did just that — and more. You

see, I happened to know that he later had a gold chain attached to the top of that twenty-dollar gold piece, which he always wore around his neck and displayed on numerous occasions — while he told its history — to all who wanted to see it, during the more than seventeen years of life that remained to him. This is true, an absolute fact; I, like two or three old timers around Lucan, have seen it and the bullet hole in its centre at least a score of times. And just before death finally did come to him, William Donnelly's last request was that his treasured gold coin be buried with him. It was!

That was all. Having given her fantastic display of marksmanship, the farewell of the Midnight Lady was brief, her departure speedy.

Wordlessly she swung into her saddle, her eyes on the wide sweep of road that lead towards London. At her "Up!" Pegasus rose on his powerful hind legs. She turned to the Donnellys to wave a brief farewell. Next came her sharp whistle; the beast returned to all fours. And then that horse tore up the road so damn fast you would have thought he had been shot from a cannon! His beauteous rider leaned slightly forward as they plunged faster, faster into that golden dawn — her long black cloak whipped out to full-length and floating behind her.

The three Donnellys watched till she disappeared into the distance.

"There she goes; like something glorious and wonderful that came from a dream and is now returning to it," William Donnelly spoke quietly. "There goes our greatest friend!"

CHAPTER SEVENTEEN

What Happened in the Graveyard

Oldsters tell grim yarns of the Roman Line,
Tales of terror, tales of fright.
Of weird things that happen far out there,
With the coming of the night.

— Old Song —

"And that is how the great feud really did end; with the triumph and vengeance of the Donnellys," concluded the old man in the graveyard. "Oh, it is a story unknown to the outside world; in fact the few who are aware of it around here can be numbered on the fingers of one hand — and they remain silent. But I tell you again, it was the Donnellys who finally won!"

By then sundown had faded, with the shades of dusk starting to steal across the sky. In fact, at that hour, a lonely graveyard was the last place in the world you would have expected to find tourists. But as though lost to time and their surroundings, for several minutes Ann and Don Graham were silent. Finally Ann broke the stillness with:

"But the Midnight Lady? What became of her? Did she ever return?"

The old man shook his head. "She never returned.

She was last seen on that distant morning when she galloped into the dawn."

All of them were still seated on the grass near the Donnelly tombstone. Ann Graham said, "I would love to have seen her." Then she got to her feet, gestured with one hand to the nearby roadway and exclaimed: "Just think — that's it out there — the Roman Line! That once so terrible road of violence, blood and death, where it all happened!"

Don Graham turned to the old man. "Thanks for your time and a thrilling story," he said. "But you know, I cannot help wondering what my friends in the States will say when I tell it to them." He reflected an instant; shrugged, chuckled and admitted: "Come to think of it, though, I guess I can. They will probably say I dreamed it all and they will laugh at me."

"You can send any skeptic this way," said the other. "I will always be willing to vouch for the truth of the story since it is true. So very true."

With the old man following his example, Don Graham got to his feet, and for the first time seemed aware that dusk had fallen. He looked around in mild surprise. Ten feet away his pretty wife was still gazing towards the road, the Roman Line, engrossed by the mere sight of it. He smiled; there had always been a bit of the romantic in Ann. Idly his own gaze went to the road, then to the left where it ran on towards the old Donnelly farm, three miles away. He wondered how many times in long distant days, the Black Donnellys had galloped over that very road as they made the air tremble with their wild shouts and wilder laughter.

All around him was the melancholy stillness of a lonely country graveyard. A graveyard where reposed the remains and tombstones of men long dead, many

of whom had experienced that terrible feud and fought
against the Donnellys. A light wind swept through surrounding trees and leaves rustled, as the thought came
to him that the inmates of some of those graves might
have even seen the fabulous Midnight Lady herself.
Many times, she too had galloped along the Roman
Line on her speedy charger, Pegasus.

Then Don Graham called to his wife: "Ann, it is
getting late."

She turned, smiling. "It is and after what we have
heard, the Roman Line is no place to be once darkness
has fallen." Her eyes went to the old man. "You told us
that some people claim this district is haunted by the
ghosts of the Donnellys. Now tell me, do you really
believe it?"

"What?" exclaimed her husband, who regarded her
for a minute, then added: "Why Ann, how can you ask
such a ridiculous question? Of course he does not
believe it. He's a sensible man and what person in
their right mind believes in ghosts?" He turned to the
old man and asked:

"Is that not so?"

But the other shook his head; not only that, his former friendly expression suddenly changed as his features became stern, his eyes hard as agate, as he
answered: "No, it is not so!" There was anger in his
voice.

He went on: "This is a strange area, Mr. Graham; a
small and bizarre world of its own, seemingly apart
from the rest of the universe, that has changed but little in the last four-score years. Yes, and since the
slaughter of the Donnellys there have been at least a
hundred people who, from time to time, have claimed
to have seen phantom riders on phantom horses —

"the ghosts of the Black Donnellys" — hurrying along the Roman Line during the blackness of the night. Now all those people could not have been liars!"

He lifted his blackthorn stick to emphasize:

"Others have told, on anniversaries of the night of the massacre, of seeing strange lights and ghostly forms hovering around the old Donnelly farm. And — whether you believe it or not — there are folks around here, even today, who will tell of occasionally hearing the distant wailing of a fiddle they claim is being played by none other than the ghost of the clubfooted William Donnelly — dead for more than sixty years! Would you care to meet some of the folks who tell this? I can take you to them!"

Ann Graham, realizing that her husband's ridicule of the supernatural had angered the old man, spoke. "Please forgive Don, sir. He — he did not stop to think. But I want to say that I believe you — I truly do." Secretly crossing her fingers, she added: "Yes — I think I believe in ghosts."

Don Graham put in: "My wife is right. I didn't stop to think; I'm sorry I said what I did." Then glibly changing the subject: "And now, suppose you let us drive you to your home? You will recall, I promised to do just that before you told us your interesting story."

The old man shook his head. "It is not necessary."

"Please," came from Ann Graham.

"It will be no trouble at all," assured her husband. We can get you there quickly, will be happy to do so; besides it will soon be dark and —."

But once more the old man shook his head and gave a deep sign before he spoke in a calm, resigned voice: "No, you do not understand; neither of you understand. I said it would not be necessary to drive me to my home nor is it. You see, I live so close; only a few steps from here!" Then the blackthorn stick was pointed directly to the sward on the right side of the nearby Donnelly tombstone — the William Donnelly plot — and the young couple heard the blood-chilling words:

"That is my home! I live exactly six feet below that patch of grass over there!"

That was all! Those were the last words they were to ever hear him speak!

A terrible expression swept across his face and the old man walked over to the Donnelly tombstone and, standing directly before it, turned and faced the Grahams. But that was not all; no, that was not quite all. Because, and for the first time, they noticed that he walked with — with a limp! And then the eyes of both of them swept down to his right trouser leg, to see exactly what they knew they would see. A clubfoot!

A sob of horror burst from Ann Graham's lips. Her husband wanted to yell, "It's William Donnelly's ghost," but the words would not leave his throat. And, at that same instant, from overhead, came a loud, "Caw — caw — caw," that raised their terrorized faces upward.

There, winging swiftly through the ever-gathering dusk, came a very large crow, carrying a violin in one claw, a bow in the other. And it made straight towards the ancient one and landed on his shoulder. But even in that wild moment, Ann Graham knew instantly that she had seen that bird before. Yes, it was the same one, the very same crow that had flown over her and then had so strangely disappeared, soon after she entered the graveyard. And with that realization came the other that caused her to throw one arm over her eyes, then shriek words that stabbed out into the surrounding dusk:

"Why it's his pet — it's Paddy! Paddy the ghost-crow!"

And the one who stood before the tombstone with the huge crow on his shoulder? He had taken the violin and bow from the bird's talons; the violin he placed under his chin, the bow was brought into position. Then, with an introductory stamping of his clubfoot for timing — the old reliable "one-and-a-two-and-a-three" he began a wild, fast and shrill rendition of the favorite jig of long ago, The Devil's Reel!

The crow on his shoulder cawed again, spread its large wings and began a rhythmical swaying — like a sort of dance!

It was too much for the young American couple. Their faces chalk-white, Don Graham grabbed his wife by the wrist, both wheeled, then began a mad, head-long dash for the road and their car, a hundred yards away. Ann sobbed hysterically while the two encircled tombstones, leaped over graves and twice plunged into patches of knee-high grass. They made the distance in record time.

Car doors were jerked open and slammed shut; lights flashed on, the motor sprang to life and the car shot away!

Behind them the wild din continued. From the darkness of that usually quite country graveyard — that silent village of the dead — came the shrill, increasingly faster and louder playing of a violin, as it repeated again and again *The Devil's Reel*. And inter-mingling with the wailing of the fiddle music — as though he sought to accompany the player — could be

heard the hard rasping screeches of Paddy the ghost-
crow:

Caw — caw — caw — caw — caw!

The ghost of the violin still plays —
For the dead sometimes return.
I know what these old eyes have seen,
I know what I did learn.
And even though a thousand years
May pass along in time:
The Ghosts of the Black Donnellys will
Still ride the Roman Line!

— Old Song —